GALVESTON BURNING

GALVESTON BURNING

A HISTORY OF THE FIRE DEPARTMENT AND MAJOR CONFLAGRATIONS

JAMES F. ANDERSON

FOREWORD BY MIKE WISKO

THE History PRESS

Published by The History Press
Charleston, SC
www.historypress.com

Opposite: Galveston Firemen's Memorial, located in front of the new Central Fire Station at Twenty-Sixth and Sealy Streets. *Author's collection.*

First published 2021

Manufactured in the United States

ISBN 9781467144650

Library of Congress Control Number: 2021943805

Notice: The information in this book is true and complete to the best of our knowledge. It is offered without guarantee on the part of the author or The History Press. The author and The History Press disclaim all liability in connection with the use of this book.

This book is dedicated to all the men and women, both past and present, of the Galveston Fire Department. They valiantly served and continue to serve the community of Galveston. Every day, they are on a mission to protect the island, its community and citizens—as well as neighboring communities—from the threat of fire, bravely risking their lives and safety to protect others. We are eternally grateful for your duty and sacrifice.

CONTENTS

FOREWORD

In this book you hold is evidence of James Anderson's passion for history and his dedication to capturing the history of the Galveston Fire Department. One of James's fondest memories as a child was the day he was made an honorary firefighter and allowed to sit on the firetruck. While James sought a different path in life, he never lost that respect and admiration for firefighters.

When I first met James, he explained that he had been researching the Galveston Fire Department (GFD) for years, and although he had found many articles, pictures and stories about the GFD, he was surprised to learn that there were no books that were just about the history of such a storied fire department. He asked me if we could assist and support his cause, and I can say that this was one of the easiest and proudest decisions I ever made as the Galveston fire chief.

The GFD has been serving the residents and visitors of this grand Texas island for more than 135 years, and the one constant that has always shined through is its dedication, passion, commitment and love for the island, which every Galveston firefighter has and will always possess. In sports, it has always been said that you must have heart to be a winner, and I can say with great pride that Galveston firefighters have heart.

While the American Fire Service has impacted our country's history in so many ways, GFD has done no different for Galveston's history. Galveston has prevailed through many catastrophic events, and the individuals who have made up the Galveston Fire Department played a huge role in every one of them. From conflagrations to hurricanes, wars and glorious festivals, Galveston firefighters have been involved. Galveston firefighters have been part of the several national incidents, such as the Murray Federal Building bombing in 1995, Hurricane Katrina in 2005, the 2011 wildfire outbreak across Texas and the historic 2018 California wildfire season. We are honored to have a book that will tell our story for years to come.

This collection of historical information was made possible through James's commitment and never-ending hard work to learn as much as he could about the GFD. He listened to and read hundreds of stories of past and present firefighters, historians and writers. He has been able to present the story of this department in a way that shines a bright light on the "pride of the island." Many family names have been associated with the GFD throughout the history of the department, and they undoubtedly will be for many years to come.

Thank you, James, for having the heart to write this book and give us this gift. And thank you to each of you who will read this book. I always considered being a Galveston firefighter the highest honor, and I, like so many other Galveston firefighters, am grateful for the opportunity.

Mike Wisko, third-generation Galveston firefighter (1988–2019)

PREFACE

Work on this book began many years ago after a conversation with Dash Beardsley, regarding a fire that hit Galveston Island. Our conversation was about the name of one of the many fires that ravaged Galveston Island. While we both had differing opinions regarding the name of the fire, in the end, we were both right; however, it was in my quest to find the name of this fire that I learned no official book had been written about the many fires that plagued our city.

I learned that numerous books discuss one or more fires but never completely in depth. While this book is in no way all-inclusive, I have sought to capture the details of the most destructive fires on the island, either by the size of the area destroyed or the final monetary cost of the destruction. This means that although many fires have been included, many others have also been omitted.

The first chapter gives a brief history of Galveston Island and the founding of the city of Galveston, along with descriptions of earlier fires known to have occurred on the island. The next chapter focuses on actions taken by the city's leaders to try to protect it from the threat of fire. The following chapter continues with a description of the creation of volunteer fire companies in the city and finally formation of the first paid fire department of Texas.

The final chapters of the book allow the reader to read about the large number of fires that ravaged the city; many of the structures that were either lost or damaged in fires; and, finally, fires that, although not large in consumption, still caused tremendous damage or even death. While I have worked hard to include as much detail as possible regarding the fires, I did run into issues where articles or records were unavailable.

In chapter 4, "The District Fires," I have purposefully broken the city of Galveston into four districts, which are then labeled the commercial district, the residential district, the wharf district and the warehouse district. As expected, the commercial district focuses on the downtown heart of the city; the residential district encompasses an area of the city that contains the Historic East End, the Lost Bayou District, the Silk Stocking District and the homes and residences that lie east of Twenty-Fifth Street. The wharf district comprises the entire Galveston Waterfront along Galveston Harbor, which is roughly bordered by Harborside Drive from Sixth Street all the way to Fifty-First Street. The warehouse district, for all intents and purposes in this book, lies to the west of Thirty-Third Street to about Fifty-Ninth Street, between Harborside Drive and Broadway, though not all warehouses were contained in this area of the city.

ACKNOWLEDGEMENTS

As an author of just one book on a single piece of Galveston's history, I want to thank the numerous authors who have written about Galveston's history. With their tomes and other sources, I have been able to share a topic that is often overlooked: the fires of Galveston Island. For a curious casual reader or a serious historian, an extensive library of information is available that covers a wide range of topics related to this fascinating island.

From the works of early historians like Amasa Turner, Dr. Joseph O. Dyer and Charles Hayes, I was able to glean what life was like in early Texas and Galveston. Early professional photographers recorded images of the island, such as P.H. Rose, the Blessing Brothers and Joseph M. Maurer, offering me a glimpse into the life of the early city. In addition to these numerous professional photographers, I am greatly indebted to the many amateur photographers who aimed their cameras, leaving behind images as records of their lives.

To the staff of Galveston and Texas History Center of the Rosenberg Library, I am greatly indebted to you for the use of the library's vast historical holdings, which assisted me in my research. I would like to give special recognition to Sean McConnell for his willingness to assist both online and over the phone. My thanks also go to Sandy Siddal of the Galveston County Museum, who searched the museum's archives and located images to enhance this manuscript; Jami Durham of the Galveston Historical Foundation, whose assistance as a friend and professional was invaluable in completing this manuscript; also the J. Levy and Termini Funeral Home, which provided an image of the original funeral home building lost in the fire.

I am indebted to Mike Wisko, Galveston's former fire chief, for his willingness to meet and discuss a book that hadn't even been written and his offer to assist me in any way possible. I am grateful for Austin Smith, who reached out and shared many valuable historical images of the Galveston Fire Department. I am also thankful for so many current and retired men and women of Galveston's fire department and their families who reached out to impart their knowledge of this worthy institution and city.

To Brian M. Davis, I would like to extend my thanks for lending me not only his ear but also his home and expertise while writing my manuscript. I want to thank Jan Johnson for her assistance locating images, imparting her knowledge and so much more. Kimber Fountain guided me along the way, to sources and people that could assist me in my endeavor. I am greatly indebted to Richard Eisenhower for not only imparting his valuable knowledge but also many wonderful images that enhanced the book for the reader. Gary Myers created the maps for this book, and for him, I am forever grateful. I am indebted to a numerous friends, including but not limited to Dale Carter, Clyde Wood and Sheri Davis, who shared my passion not only for Galveston but also for the sources and images used in this book.

Numerous images used throughout this manuscript came from my own collection; however, others were obtained from the Galveston and Texas History Center at the Rosenberg Library, the Galveston County Museum, the Library of Congress's Historic American Building Survey, the New York Public Library and the Dolph Briscoe Center for American History, as well as other private collections.

INTRODUCTION

Galveston, a barrier island, sits on the northwest coast of the Gulf of Mexico and runs parallel with the Texas coastline, sitting about fifty miles to the southeast of Houston, Texas. The city of Galveston on the northeastern tip of the island fronts the bay of the same name, forming one half of the area known as Bolivar Roads. A channel runs between Galveston Island and Bolivar Peninsula, named for Simon Bolivar, or the "Liberator," of Venezuela.

This island, though small in stature, has hosted a number of men and women who had a hand in the development of the island and city. These men and women, many unknown and not-so-famous, traveled to this small island—some staying to carve out a life for themselves and others who would merely pass through the port to lands farther inland. Each of these people left their mark on this city, creating the island community we know today.

The original city, located on Galveston Bay, was a large tract of land acquired by Michel B. Menard in 1833. This league and labor of land was laid out with intersecting avenues and streets creating a grid pattern. The city grew from the protected natural harbor and stretched across the island to the gulf. Starting at the harbor, the grid consisted of avenues that ran approximately east to west and streets that ran north to south.

Avenues were lettered alphabetically starting with A and so forth, terminating at the beach. Today Avenue A is officially known as Harborside

Drive. Avenue B, referred to as "Strand Street," got its name from jeweler Michael W. Shaw, who wanted a more prestigious address and so chose Strand Street, like the street in London. Eventually, other businesses soon adopted the name, and the street's name was later formally changed. Avenue C, formally known as Ship's Mechanic's Row, is usually shortened to Mechanic Street. Avenue D, also known as Market Street, is the location of the city's original market. Avenue E was named Postoffice Street, as the original post office was located on this street.[1] Over time, the post office was relocated, but the street has kept the name. Avenue F, or Church Street, was named for Saint Mary's Cathedral and the large number of churches located along the street. Avenue G, originally named Menard Street, was later changed to Winnie Street after Gilbert Winnie. Avenue H was originally named Williams Street and was later changed to Ball Street in honor of George Ball, benefactor of Ball High School. Avenue I, originally named McKinney Street, was renamed Sealy Street in honor of John Sealy. Avenue J is formally known as Broadway Street because it is a wide thoroughfare that cuts across the city. Avenues K, L and M were originally named Jones, Borden and Baker, respectively; however, these names were later removed and are no longer being used. Avenue N, known as Ursuline Street, was named for the ornate Ursuline Convent and School that was located here between Twenty-Fifth and Twenty-Seventh Streets. After construction of the seawall, a grand promenade was established; over time, it was named Seawall Boulevard.

The cross streets of Galveston are numbered sequentially; though very few of these streets have official names, a few do have secondary names. Twenty-First Street is known as Center Street, and Twenty-Third Street is known as Tremont Street. Twenty-Fifth Street later became known as Bath Avenue due to its connection with the "bathing" area on the gulf. On San Jacinto Day, April 21, 1900, with the dedication of the Texas Heroes Monument, the street was renamed Rosenberg Street in honor of Henry Rosenberg, one of Galveston's largest philanthropists.

The intersection of these streets and avenues created a grid pattern composed of blocks. The blocks to the east of Broadway Street comprised one regular city block; however, the blocks on the west side of Broadway Street comprised ten acres and were designated as out-lots. These out-lots were sold to farms, estates and businesses; however, as the population increased, these blocks were cut in half by "half streets," which cut these out-lots into regular city blocks.

With a city of this size growing rapidly, fire protection was essential for the city's survival. So, within the following chapters, the reader will be introduced to this city, its citizens and the fires that plagued it, creating an urgent need for a paid fire department and improved fire safety.

1
HISTORY OF GALVESTON

Today, when one arrives on Galveston Island, it's hard to imagine that this large, populated tourist city was once an uncharted barrier island. However, it is this Galveston, originally a small part of vast land holdings of Spain, where our story takes place. Early Spanish explorers traveling to the New World came near to this area to see and map the newly acquired holdings of Spain and to search for supposed cities of gold. Rene-Robert Cavelier Sieur de La Salle, though he never once set foot on it, would tell of it in his journal and his mapping of the Texas coast.

Another Spanish explorer who was not searching for the island found himself entrenched in its history. Around July 1528, Álvar Núñez Cabeza de Vaca set out on an expedition with nearly three hundred men and forty horses from Cuba to settle and colonize these lands for the Spanish Crown. Lost and totally misdirected, Cabeza de Vaca and his men built five rafts to hold fifty men each. These men then sailed from the coast of Florida on September 22, 1528, looking for a settlement of their own countrymen. Several months later, on November 6, 1528, a terrible storm washed Cabeza de Vaca and his few men onto the shore of Galveston Island, or close to it.

In Cabeza de Vaca's time, Galveston Island was a barren spit of sand on the edge of Texas with very little in the way of vegetation, and it was devoid of life, except for hundreds of snakes and the Karankawa Natives. Cabeza de Vaca would survive his ordeal on the island and return to Spain; however, most of his three-hundred-man crew died. His story, recorded in his diary, was later published in 1541 and again in 1551.

Left: Rene-Robert Cavelier Sieur de La Salle. *Right*: Bernardo de Galvez. *Public domain.*

Early Spanish maps labeled the island as Isla de Culberas, or "Snake Island," named for the hundreds of snakes that made the island their home. Other names, such as Isla de Mulhaldo, or "Isle of Misfortune," would be coined by Cabeza de Vaca, who had been shipwrecked on the island. But the true name of Galveston wouldn't come until July 23, 1786, when José de Evia was sent by Spanish colonial governor and general Bernardo de Galvez to chart the Texas coast to New Orleans. José de Evia would name the bay and the island for Bernardo de Galvez himself.

In September 1816, Michel Luis Aury, a French pirate, sailed into Galveston Bay; his objective was to take the position as resident commissioner of Galveston Island. He declared the island a port of Mexico, established his own government and began to direct his profitable privateering operations from this strategic point. Henry Perry, a man who had tried to invade Texas from Bolivar Peninsula and failed, later joined Aury with one hundred additional men. In late 1816, General Xavier Mina, a young Spanish insurgent, would join Aury and Perry with two hundred men to organize an invasion of Mexico. Both men sought to gain access to the Mexican silver mines and to take control of Florida from Spain.

Due to a disagreement on April 15, 1817, the men left Galveston to attack the Port of Tampico, having destroyed all their huts in Galveston.

Although they took Tampico without a fight, the three men could not cooperate with one another. Mina and Perry took the fight farther inland, and Aury decided to cut his losses and return to Galveston and his profitable privateering enterprise.

Upon Aury's arrival back in Galveston in October 1817, he found that Privateer Jean Laffite and his men, the "Baratarians," had moved in and taken control of the island and his camp. After finding the Laffite brothers on the island, Aury chose to leave without a fight and move his base of operations elsewhere.

Jean and his brother, Pierre Lafitte, already very familiar with Galveston Island, chose to return to the island after they were ousted from New Orleans. Laffite's early history is a bit muddled; believed to be born in France, possibly Paris, he left France for the West Indies. Other accounts state that Laffite took a wife, and while aboard a ship, possibly on their honeymoon, he was attacked by the Spanish. Laffite and his new wife were abandoned on a deserted island, where his wife died. Laffite survived this ordeal and later took vengeance on the Spanish, attacking their vessels and taking its plunder. Whatever the true story may be, Jean did settle in New Orleans, and he and his brother, Pierre, would open a blacksmith shop, a front for his pirating and smuggling business. Jean and his group of men would prowl the Gulf Coast and hide their ships and bounty along Barataria Bay, close to New Orleans.

In 1815, Jean assisted the Americans in the Battle of New Orleans, where they once and for all showed the British America was no longer a weak nation. Due to Laffite's assistance, America won the war, and the British no longer occupied American soil. Shortly after the war, Laffite was named an American Patriot for his assistance, and his status was elevated by the American government to that of a privateer.

After the war, while attending a lavish party held at the French Exchange, Laffite approached a group of men, including General Andrew Jackson and Governor William C. Claiborne, a man who had tried, many times, to remove him from Louisiana. Governor Claiborne, speaking to the general, asked, "Do you know Mr. Laffite, general?" Instead of stating that he did or that he had helped in the battle, no one spoke a word; several of the men turned their backs on Laffite, this being their silent way of denouncing him. This type of treatment upset Laffite greatly; within weeks, it became apparent to Laffite that his time in New Orleans was over and that it was time to move on.

Laffite came to Galveston on March 23, 1817, while Aury still controlled the port. On April 7, 1817, Aury and Mina sailed away from the island. Laffite

Jean Lafitte, Telfer woodcutting. *Courtesy of Dale Olsen.*

stated in his diary that, on April 8, he and his men took control of Aury's settlement and named officers and an administration. Aury later returned to Galveston Island to resupply; however, finding he no longer had control of the island, he left for good.

Laffite established his settlement, Campeche, on the bay side of Galveston. The town, rudimentary at best, was composed of buildings made of various planks, logs and canvases with thatched roofs; however, at its height, the town boasted a population of nearly one thousand people. Actual descriptions of Laffite's "Maison Rouge" are conflicting. While several reports of the structure do exist, the most credible of them never mention the building being painted red.[2] Whatever the case may be, Laffite's time in Galveston was well spent; he entertained lavishly, developed Campeche and continued to amass his wealth and grow his enterprise. However, his luck was soon to run out.

In the fall of 1819, two cruisers commissioned by Laffite set sail out of Galveston under specific orders to attack Spanish vessels. Captain Brown decided to defy those orders and instead sailed to Louisiana, where he attacked and plundered a plantation, taking all that his men could carry. Cruising nearby, the U.S. revenue schooner *Lynx* saw the whole ordeal. Brown and his men set sail for Galveston with the *Lynx* in hot pursuit. Upon Brown's arrival and after finding out what had happened, Laffite hanged Brown from the gallows and had his men flogged and turned over to the Americans. He then threw a party for the crew of the *Lynx*, sparing no expense. It seemed that tragedy had been averted; however, early in 1821, the USS *Enterprise* sailed into Galveston Harbor; the captain gave Laffite orders to leave Galveston Island along with all of his men. Laffite asked for an extension long enough to clean up his affairs and to prepare to leave. About two months later, the *Enterprise* sailed back into Galveston Bay. Laffite, true to his word, had just completed loading his ship, dispersed his men and was prepared to sail. Laffite held a lavish party for the men aboard the *Enterprise* and, that evening, set the town ablaze. While Campeche burned to the ground, Laffite's ship, the *Jupiter*, sailed out of Galveston Harbor, into the open waters of the gulf and the pages of history and mystery.

After Laffite burned the town to the ground, Galveston Island returned to the place it had been before: a barren land populated with huts, pirates, Natives and a Mexican customs official, who took over the newly created national port of Mexico. In 1833, Michel Branamour Menard would purchase the title for Galveston from the Mexican government through an agent named Juan Nepomuceno Seguin for $50,000. Although he had clear title of the land in 1833, the fight for Texas's independence was on the horizon, and the establishment of the city was still a ways off. After the battle for Texas's independence on April 21, 1836, Menard's deed was contested. Although he did own clear title to the land, it had been purchased from the Mexican government but now belonged to the new Republic of Texas, therefore nullifying the original deed. On December 3, 1836, Menard again purchased the labor and a league of land on the east end of Galveston Island; this parcel contained the earlier settlements of Aury and Laffite. John D. Groesbeck was hired in 1837 to survey the land, which brothers Thomas and Gail Borden then laid out in the grid pattern containing the blocks and lots of today's modern city.

Juan N. Seguin. *Author's collection.*

Gail Borden Sr. *Author's collection.*

Before the city of Galveston was established, early settlers began arriving on Galveston Island just east of the present-day city, in an area from roughly Sixth Street to Seventeenth Street and from the water's edge, including portions of Strand and Mechanic Streets. These early settlers came from a small village in Maine known as Saccarappa on the Presumpscot River; it was named for a Native word that meant "falling toward the rising sun," as the river's eastern course had a number of waterfalls. Upon their arrival,

Thomas F. McKinney.

Left: Thomas F. McKinney. *Right*: Leo N. Levi. *Author's collection.*

these early settlers began to establish their community of the "Saccarappa," naming it after their Maine village. They brought with them artisans, craftsmen and a number of wooden structures made from white pine that had been sawn, assembled, disassembled and then rebuilt on Galveston Island. The community, which only lasted for about ten to fifteen years, sat to the eastern edge of the early city of Galveston, boasting a hotel and the very first wharf to be built on Galveston Bay, commissioned by Amasa Turner. The very first court was held on the island in this community; though, over time, most of the residents eventually decided to move to the rival community of Galveston to the west.[3]

By January 25, 1838, Menard had received the quitclaim title to Galveston. By April 13, the Galveston City Company had been established by several other persons through their trustees, such as Levi Jones, William R. Johnson and Thomas M. Green, with the issuance of one thousand shares of stock for $1,000 each. The purchasers of the shares and holders of the stock became the "Galveston City Company." After the Galveston City Company was organized, a board of five directors was appointed and committed to the management of the property of the company. The first board of directors was composed of Michel B. Menard, president; Thomas F. McKinney; Samuel May Williams; Moseley Baker; and John R. Allen. A week later, the first public sale of lots began on the island. The city began to develop,

Early view of Galveston, circa 1845. *Author's collection.*

boasting a population of about 580 when Sam Houston, the first president of the newly formed republic, signed into law the creation of Galveston County from a portion of Brazoria County on May 15, 1838.

On March 18, 1839, the city was officially established, and on February 5, 1841, the Galveston City Company incorporated through an act of congress within the republic. On January 1, 1842, Menard conveyed control of the city to the president, directors and stockholders of the Galveston City Company.

With the development of the new city, a building boom began on the island, and with growth came the possibility of disaster. Records of early fires on the island are pretty much nonexistent, as structures of the time were remarkably simple frame buildings with no intrinsic value to the owners. This being the case, little to no insurance was held on these buildings, and not much in the way of early fire prevention was done. At the start of the Civil War, very few homes or buildings of substantial construction existed on the island. Some of the earliest surviving examples of these early structures

Menard family home, 1838. *Author's collection.*

are Michel B. Menard's home (1838), Samuel May Williams's home (1838), the Powhatan Hotel (1847), Wilbur Cherry's home (1852) and St. Joseph's Church (1859).

By the 1850s, Galveston's population had soared to over four thousand, and men began building more substantial structures on the island; however, these buildings were few and far between compared to the number of wooden structures on the island.

An early article published by Dr. Greensville Dowell in the *Galveston Medical Journal* gave a description of the city in its early days.[4]

> *The present city is mostly east of Bath Avenue, which is the centre street running north and south upon the map. West of the avenue and north of Broadway is a large pond, in which is daily deposited all manner of filth. This pond forms the head of McKinney's Bayou—a natural sewer—which, when flooded with fresh water, bursts into the gulf several miles below the city.... The houses are mostly of wood, of all styles of architecture.... The alleys are the receptacles of all the filth of the house yard and kitchen.... The yards of many of our citizens are as bad as the alleys.*[5]

St. Joseph's Church, 1859. *Author's collection.*

View of Galveston, 1850. *Author's collection.*

The earliest known fire occurred just after the founding of the city on the east end of the island in a hotel created from an old steamboat that had washed up on the shore. The fire began in the kitchen of the hotel. When the residents were alerted to the fire, a call was put out for a "bucket brigade" to attempt to contain it and put it out. A bucket brigade, just as it sounds, was a group of nearby volunteers or bystanders who would grab buckets and form two lines from the nearest water source, such as the bay, the ocean or cisterns. These buckets of water would then be thrown on the fire until it was eventually extinguished. These bucket brigades, though rudimentary at best, were, at the time, the best way of putting out a fire.

Later fires would eventually lead to the development of a volunteer fire department. One such fire broke out on the premises of the William and Armstrong Brothers' Building in a back structure. The fire began just before daylight and had consumed a good portion of the interior before it finally broke through the roof of the building and was discovered. The building, at the time, was filled with schoolbooks and stationery. After the fire was put out, the loss was estimated to cost about $1,000. The strangest part of this fire was that there was no stove, fireplace or any conceivable source, unless it had been intentionally set. An article in the *Galveston Daily News* reported on this fire and stated, "Our readers are generally aware that nearly every fire of late has taken place in the night and during our severest 'northers,' and the evidence concludes that they have been the work of incendiaries."

While there were a number of fires during that period, most were small and easily put out with little loss.[6] The largest fire at this time occurred on January 12, 1858, at a frame structure used by nuns of Saint Ursula's-by-the-Sea at the corner of Twenty-Sixth Street and Avenue N. Around noon, just after the completion of their lunch, all the nuns stood in the community room, waiting to be released for their recreational time. Before the prayer could be said, a commotion was heard outside the window, and a white-faced nun ran into the door, shouting, "Our dormitory is on fire." When they looked out the window, huge clouds of black smoke could be seen billowing from the building. Reverend Mother Chantal gave orders: "Get buckets and wet blankets! Let us do what we can." The nuns raced toward the dormitory, trying frantically to put out the fire, while many priceless treasures, pieces of furniture and everyday items were carried out and piled in the yard.

Bird's-eye view of Galveston, 1870. *Courtesy of the New York Public Library.*

Miriam and Ira D. Wallach Division of Art, Prints and Photographs Collection, New York Public Library, "Galveston, Texas. [Bird's-eye view of businesses and view of harbor.]," New York Public Library Digital Collections, www.digitalcollections.nypl.org.

Though the fire department was on its way, the sandy soil and ruts in the road made it extremely difficult to get to the fire in time. By the time the fire department had arrived, the fire had completely destroyed the building and left the nuns looking for another home.

Throughout Galveston's occupation during the Civil War, the number of fires increased dramatically on the island. The cause of many of the fires was thought to be arson, though the actual person or persons who set the fires was never caught. One of these early fires was discovered on May 27, 1861, and caused the loss of Briggs's and Yard's store and damage to nearby property. The fire was first discovered in the post office; an alarm was sounded, and thankfully, due to the fact that it was a small fire, it was easily put out with a bucket of water. Thinking the fire had started in the post office on the corner of Market and Twenty-Second Streets, bystanders took precious time to determine the fire was still blazing in the back of back of Briggs's and Yard's store located on Market Street between Twenty-Second and Twenty-Third Streets. When the fire was found, it was already in progress, consuming the buildings. By the time the fire department arrived, the building that contained the store and the adjoining wooden buildings had been destroyed. It was estimated that the loss of the building as well as its contents would cost well above $2,000; however, due to the war, the insurance, which was from the North, was not paid.

On May 2, 1862, three houses owned by Mr. Thacker on Market Street were completely destroyed. The fire had started in the back part of the property that was owned by Philip Gildersleeve. This fire was very suspicious in origin, as Gildersleeve was not even in town at the time and no fire had been used that day in the dwelling. Around December 11, 1866, a fire was reported to have damaged the building constructed by brothers William and Joseph Hendley. It was stated sparks and pieces of the burning building were carried several blocks away and ignited the roofs of several other buildings, including the Odd Fellows Hall and the bulletin office. On December 17, 1866, the business of J.H.F. Chapman and L.J. Duffield and the Masonic hall on Postoffice and Tremont Streets were destroyed by fire.

On August 14, 1867, a fire broke out in the barbershop of Nicholas V. Lacroix on Center Street, opposite the Washington Hotel.[7] The building, which was damaged, thankfully had most of its furnishings saved due to the assistance of J. Dumas, who kept the bar next door. The tailor shop next door was damaged; however, little was lost. The property itself belonged to Christopher Fox, and the damage was estimated to cost between $5,000 and

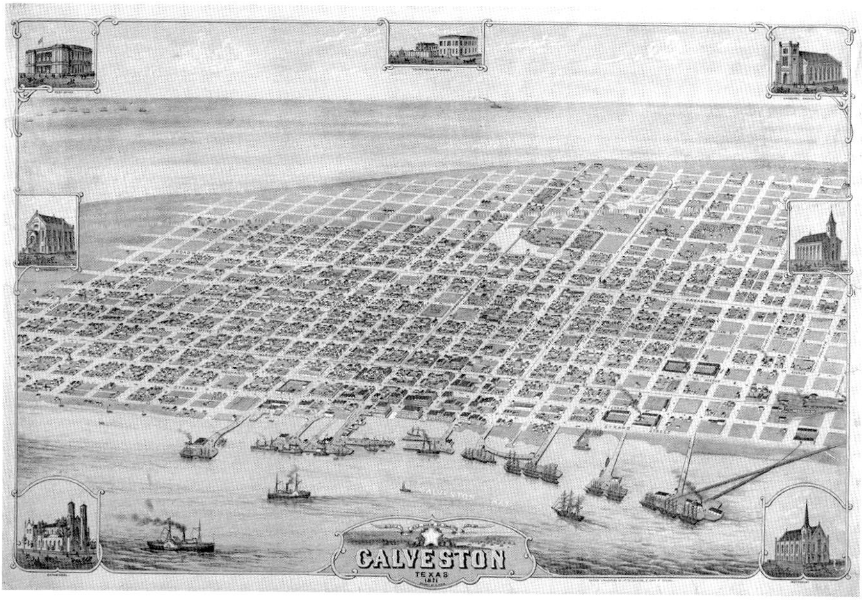

Map of Galveston, 1871. *Author's collection.*

$6,000. Mr. LeCroix's money, about $2,000 of which was insured, was not released to him until the fire was investigated.

As Galveston began to grow, its population began to expand; its original population in 1838 was 580. By 1870, Galveston was already boasting a population of nearly 13,838.[8] With the rise in population and the increased number of more substantial homes and businesses, destruction by fire became much more of a threat to the city.

From the 1870s until the formation of the paid Galveston Fire Department, a number of fires hit the island, causing havoc and destruction to the city. Due to the many fires and the rising cost to insure buildings in Galveston, many of Galveston's merchants and citizens rallied for a paid fire department.

2

GALVESTON CITY IMPROVEMENTS

Located on a barrier island, the city of Galveston has faced a number of major threats, including illnesses, wars and natural disasters. However, long before the city of Galveston was firmly established on the banks of the Gulf of Mexico, fire prevention was a vital piece of its growth. The early city's forefathers knew for their city to survive, they would need to establish a constitution and ordinances to protect it from threats on all fronts.

The early limits for the city of Galveston placed the city between Seventh and Thirty-First Streets, from the gulf to the bay. With city lots being sold and streets being laid out for the city, the council found it needed to move structures from the established thoroughfares, as early residents built structures wherever they saw fit. Next, the city focused on establishing itself as a port city. In 1839, the Galveston City Company began improving the city, with the first wharf, Palmetto Wharf, being built at the foot of Twenty-Fourth Street. Soon to follow was Kuhn's Wharf at Eighteenth Street and then, in 1840, the Central Wharf at Twenty-First Street. Over time, Parson's Wharf was established at Twenty-First Street; Merchant's Wharf at Sixteenth Street; the Brick Wharf at Twentieth Street; the Commercial Wharf at Twenty-Fifth Street; Labadie's Wharf at Twenty-Sixth Street; and the Western Wharf at Twenty-Seventh Street. Bean's Wharf was later added to the rear of block 689 of the city.

In 1854, the Galveston Wharf Company was established to control the waterfront and several of its wharves.

Galveston City Hall, 1890, designed by Alfred Muller. *Author's collection.*

CITY MARKET

The Galveston City Company also planned to construct a building to house the city government. In 1846, John Seabrook Sydnor, the then mayor, proposed an idea to construct a combined building for the city market and city hall. Originally, a site was chosen on the north side of Market Street, between Twentieth and Twenty-First Streets. However, those lots were sold, and the proceeds were used to purchase three lots on the west side of Twentieth Street, which extended from Market to Strand Streets. The original building was 120 feet long and 40 feet wide, and it was about a story and a half in height. The bottom half of the building contained the stalls of the city's market, and the upper stories contained the offices of the city. On the north end of the building was a belfry, a tower and bell used to sound alarms and strike the hours of the day.

Early on, the back side of the market building housed equipment used by the fire department. As the city developed, in 1898, a more substantial building of stone was designed by Alfred Muller. This building was an impressive two-story structure with a tower, ornamental towers and statuary gracing the edifice.

FIRE ORDINANCES

While the city of Galveston was still in its infancy, the early founders knew that in order for their city to survive, a constitution with ordinances was needed. On April 8, 1839, the first city ordinance was passed concerning the disposal of dead animals in the streets. Other ordinances would soon follow, including those protecting the city from fire.

Early ordinances placed strict regulations on fires and lamps to keep the city from burning to the ground due to the carelessness of its residents. Other ordinances focused on providing equipment for extinguishing fires, including one that stated every home was required to have a fire bucket in every room of the dwelling or in any establishment where a fire might be found.

Although many of Galveston's buildings were spread far apart, most if not all were wood-framed buildings, which were highly flammable. All parts of these structures, from the floors to the roof, were made entirely of wood; therefore, the threat of destruction by fire was one that was faced on a daily basis. And even though the city was surrounded by water on all sides, sources of water near the areas where fires might occur were rare. Therefore, it was imperative that ordinances be put into place to assist with the extinguishing of fires.

The following ordinances regarding the "prevention or extinguishment of fires" were published in the 1859 Galveston City Directory, printed by Willard Richardson:

> *False alarms forbid; bells not allowed to be rung except in the case of fires, faster than one stroke per second, firearms, crackers, rockets not allowed to be discharged near any house within the city. Fires not allowed in yards, alleys. Stovepipes not allowed unless conducted through flues or chimneys; and when passing through wooden partitions, they must be enclosed in a stone or earthen crock, with a space of one inch between said pipe and crock.*
>
> *The owner or occupant of any house in the city is required to keep at least one fire bucket for every room on his premises where a fire is kept, said bucket holding two and a half gallons of water and marked with the owner's name or initials. No person is allowed to keep at one time over twenty-five pounds of powder in his store or house, but all persons are required to store their powder in the public powder house.*
>
> *A company called the Fire Brigade is organized under the direction of the mayor, consisting of no less than thirty men and commanded by the mayor, assisted by the wardens.*[9]

In time, these ordinances came to include occupancy requirements of certain buildings, requirements to provide alternate means of escape should a fire occur, as well as requirements to provide smoke-detecting devices, fire suppression systems and many other systems that helped limit the destruction of property or loss of life.

FIRE LIMITS

The 1859 city directory stated that, as of October 1, 1855, "none but fireproof buildings" were allowed to be erected between Bath Avenue and Nineteenth Street and from the bay to Avenue C, under penalty of $100 for every day each building continued to stand in a fire limit. If there was an existing structure within these bounds, then repairs were allowed to be made to the structure.

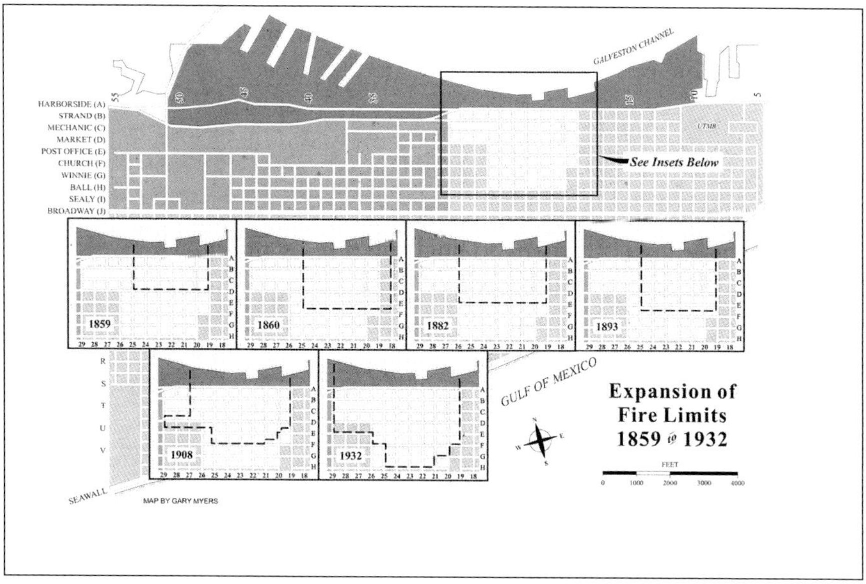

Expansion of the city of Galveston fire limits. *Courtesy of Gary Meyers.*

The first big fire to hit the city occurred in 1858, when a major conflagration struck a number of buildings on Mechanic, Strand and Twenty-Second Streets. Consequently, in that year, the city amended the ordinance, stating no longer was a wooden structure, such as a building, shed or such, allowed to be constructed within the fire limits. It also required any building given a temporary permission of construction by the city also be removed no more than one year after it was constructed.

On June 10, 1859, the city ordinances were once again updated, and at this time, the fire limits were once again extended westward to Eighteenth Street and southward to the alley between Postoffice and Church Streets. Verbiage added at this time denied permission for wooden structures to be moved within the fire limits or for existing wooden structures within the fire limits to be expanded.

By 1875, the limits had been adjusted to include the area between Avenue A to the north, the alley between Avenue E and Avenue F to the south, Eighteenth Street to the east and Twenty-Fifth Street to the west. By 1932, the fire limits included the property between Nineteenth to Twenty-Ninth Streets and all parts of the city between Avenue A and Avenue H.

Fire tower, 1868, First Ward Market. *Author's collection.*

FIRE TOWER AND BELL

In 1868, a neighborhood market was built with the stipulation that it contain a bell tower to alert citizens of a fire. The building was erected on the northwest corner of Eleventh and Mechanic Streets and remained in that location until 1904, when it was razed. While the tower did help warn residents of fires, it was also used to guide ships safely into harbor and to announce the start of the workday at 7:00 a.m. Early on, the bell tower was tolled twice when a fire or signs of a fire were detected in order to warn residents and to call the "bucket brigade to the fire."

FIREPROOF BUILDING MATERIALS

Aside from the fire limits, early code enforcements were established to protect buildings from fire. These early codes and ordinances focused less on occupant safety and more on the protection of the building and property. Design standards, such as moving from building with wood to more "fire resistant" materials, such as brick or stone, helped to reduce the loss of a structure. Ordinances that focused on the proper installation of flues for stoves and chimneys in buildings, as well as the storage of flammable materials in these structures, were also put into place.

While these ordinances did decrease the flammability of buildings, not all complied with these early standards. Many of the buildings in the commercial district were still made mostly of wood or flammable materials and were near buildings made of supposed "fireproof" materials. Over time, the destruction of these early buildings due to fire paved the way for more substantial brick and stone buildings to take their place.

Of all the design requirements placed on the citizens of Galveston, only one would come back to haunt them: the requirement to replace wooden shingles with slate tile. During the height of the 1900 hurricane, these shingles were hurled from the buildings at a high velocity. Many of these flying shingles caused severe injuries to those who were trying to escape the storm; however, to others, these pieces of shrapnel brought immediate death. Shortly after the storm of September 8, 1900, the requirement of residents to use slate shingles was repealed.

After 1900, building codes began to focus more on the safety of the occupants as well and began requiring that buildings provide adequate safety features, such as fire alarms, emergency exits and smoke control. Over time, design standards were improved, focusing instead on the number of people allowed in a space at any given time, as well as requiring the inclusion of interior sprinklers and such.

STREET PAVING

Another threat to the city was the composition of its streets. Early Galveston streets were unpaved and consisted of sandy soil. In the event of a fire, trying to traverse the shifting nature of the sand made getting to a fire in a reasonable amount of time nearly impossible. And many times, early fire equipment would get bogged down in the sand. Several axles were broken

Market Street, circa 1907. The street was paved in brick. *Author's collection.*

due to many ruts created by the sand. Over time, Galveston sought to alleviate the issue by trying to pave a number of its roads.

As of July 1, 1871, the ordinances of the city declared that the streets be paved with clam shells no less than six inches in depth, and the main thoroughfares of the city were to be paved no more than fifteen inches in depth. These main thoroughfares included Avenue B, or Strand Street, from Fifteenth Street to Twenty-Ninth Street; Avenue C, or Ships Mechanic's Row, from Fifteenth Street to Thirty-Fourth Street; Twenty-Third Street, from the bay to the gulf; and Eighteenth Street to Twenty-Ninth Street, between Strand Street and Mechanic Street. One final street left to be paved was Thirty-Third Street, between Mechanic Street and Market Street.

By 1874, the city aldermen began to look at paving the very heavily traveled Market Street. While oyster shell had been widely used before, the aldermen began looking for something much more substantial to hold up to the heavy traffic. It was determined that large blocks of creosoted pine would be used to pave this thoroughfare. The creosoted wood blocks would remain in place on Market Street well into the early

1900s, when bricks would replace them. These early efforts to improve the quality of the streets using shell, wooden blocks, bricks and eventually concrete and asphalt increased the response time of the fire companies to the fires, thereby decreasing the destruction of buildings and property in the city.

FIRE INSURANCE MAPS

As a researcher, one of the single most important items used in research is a map. A map not only gives you the layout of the city, but it can also provide you with details, such as the ownership of a particular parcel of land or the total area encompassed within certain boundaries. One such map that was and continues to be a valuable resource not only to researchers but also to city planners is the Sanborn Fire Insurance map. The Sanborn

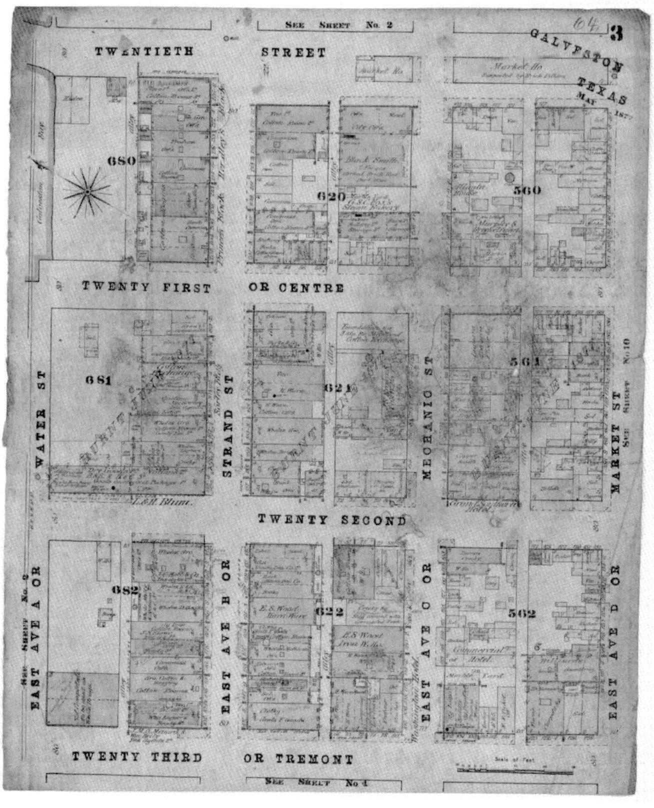

Sanborn Fire Insurance Map, 1877. *Courtesy of the Dolph Briscoe Center for American History.*

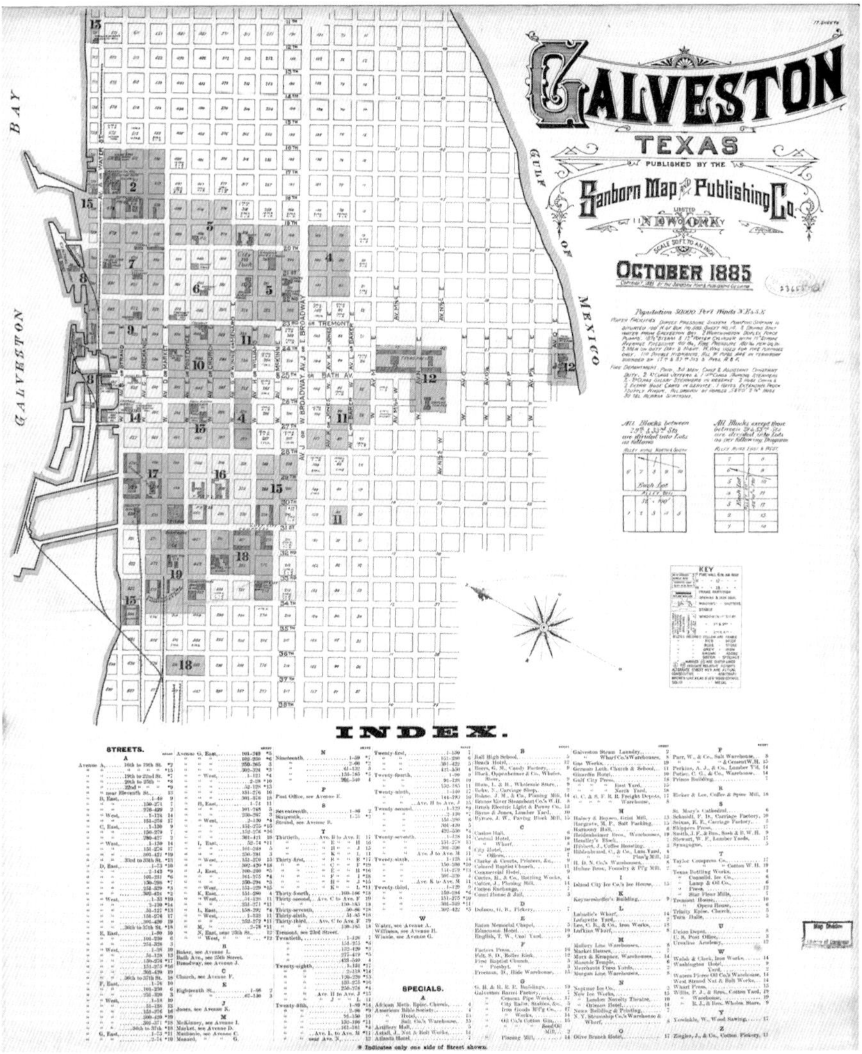

Sanborn Fire Insurance Map, 1885. *Courtesy of the Dolph Briscoe Center for American History.*

Company was established in 1867 by D.A. Sanborn and has continued to publish and update maps of every major American city since that time. These maps were originally created for the fire insurance industry for risk assessment purposes.

These maps were invaluable to the city, as they documented not just the buildings within the fire limits of the city but also the materials the structures were composed of, the height of the structures, the functions of the structures and the locations of any lot lines. The maps also included additional structures that were a part of each building or on the property, as well as locations of cisterns and wells on the properties. And in many instances, the owners of the land or structures, as well as the names of whatever businesses occupied the structures, were listed on the map. Galveston researchers are fortunate in that these maps from 1877, 1885, 1889, 1912 and 1947 are available online for their use.

FIRE TELEGRAPH SYSTEM

In July 1876, a fire alarm telegraph system was installed that allowed for better signaling of the fire companies should a fire start in areas where the alarms were placed. This system was created to replace the aging and crude fire watchtower method.

There were a total of twenty alarm boxes set up: ten east of Twenty-Second Street and ten west of Twenty-Second Street. These boxes were attached by twelve miles of wires, which had been strung between 196 poles throughout the residential district and on top of the buildings in the business district.

The system employed two large bells, which sounded the alarm; one for the east end, in the Second Ward Market House, which had been built between Eleventh Street and Mechanic Streets, and the other was located at St. John's Methodist Church, on Broadway Street and Bath Avenue in the western district. Along with the bells, there were nine gongs placed in the firehouses. A report was written at the time the fire alarm telegraph system was established stating that a gong was placed in the residence of Fire Chief Martin A. Davey and another was placed in his saloon on Strand Street.

The entire system began at Tenth Street and went as far north as Thirty-Third Street, and it stretched from Strand Street to Avenue O½. Each of the boxes in the system were numbered, with the smaller numbers located in the business district and the larger numbers located in the less populated residential areas.

On July 4, 1876, with the system complete, the city waited with bated breath to find out how the system would work. Precisely at 8:00 a.m., L.H. Firman, the western general agent of the American District Telegraph Company, the designated timekeeper for the occasion, sounded the alarm from box no. 34 at the corner of Bath Avenue and Avenue I, at the residence of Alderman Isidore Dyer. Mr. Firman recorded the arrivals of each of

Above: A view of the chief's office showing the Gamewell fire alarm system, city hall. *Author's collection.*

Left: Racing to a call, circa 1910. *Courtesy of the Galveston County Museum.*

the companies, noting their times in the log. The first to the alarm was the Phoenix Hook and Ladder Company No. 2, which made the run in one minute and thirty seconds, while Hope Fire Company No. 4 came in last at five minutes. In all, the eight companies of the city of Galveston made the run in record time; however, it was to be noted that Hope Fire Company, the company that came in last, had traveled the unpaved streets of Galveston and made the best running time of the day.

Right after the test, Mr. L.H. Firman paid the Galveston Fire Department a high compliment when he told Chief Martin A. Davey, "With all his experience with the fire departments of the large cities of the country, he never saw the time made by the Galveston fire ladders beaten." While the alarm system was a definite improvement over the watchtower, it, too, had its downfalls. First, it still relied on someone to pull the switch to initiate the alarm. Second, the alarms were quite a distance from one another, so precious time was lost trying to set the alarm and wait for the fire companies to get there.

YELLOW FEVER, SANITATION AND THE CITY WATERWORKS

In discussing the creation of the city's waterworks, readers must first go back to the early days of Galveston. The early city did not look much like a city, with small dwellings sporadically placed about the island, narrow sandy streets and crude wooden wharves that stretched hundreds of feet from the shore, into the shallow waters of the bay. Yes, early Galveston looked vastly different from the modern city we see today. At high tide, ships rode high on the waters and sailed over the bar out into the gulf; however, in low tide, many of these ships sat low in the muddy bottoms of the harbor, being unloaded by horses and wagons that came out into the shallow waters along the ships to unload and carry the cargo in.

Closer to the shore, the marshes formed, and as the tide went out, they became breeding grounds for numerous mosquitoes, which plagued the residents, especially along the waterfront and Strand Street. However, these were not the only locations where the mosquitoes would nest. Small freshwater lakes farther inland would fill with water during infrequent rainstorms, and small depressions across the city would puddle with water. As the tides receded and the rains passed, much of this water receded and left stagnated depressions or pools filled with the pollution from the yards, alleys and streets of the city.

The most dreaded of the city's epidemics, yellow fever, came as a single case to Galveston in 1837. By 1839, yellow fever had become a full-blown epidemic, terrorizing the city and its residents, leaving nearly 250 dead from its population of about 1,500. Dr. Ashbel Smith cared for the afflicted, looking for clues to tie the victims together.

IN A LETTER WRITTEN to his friend Anthony Lagrove on December 27, 1839, Dr. Nicholas Labadie wrote:

> *The epidemic which visited our infant city in October and November became a scourge to me; all my household became attacked at one time; my two little daughters recovered, my carpenter died Sunday night, my clerk of the black vomit expired on Monday night, and my wife breathed her last about two hours after Nov. 5th of the congestive fever.*[10]

While the disease, in fact, hit the city again in 1844, 1847, 1854, 1858 and 1864, the final yellow fever epidemic hit Galveston in 1867. At the time, the role the mosquito played in the transmission of the disease was not yet understood. For many doctors, city officials and citizens, at the beginning of an epidemic onslaught, sanitation measures were put in place to clean up the city.

One of the early sanitation measures used to clean up the city included a city waterworks. Every citizen, including those in the fire department, relied heavily on any and all handy water sources. For many years, the citizens of Galveston knew collection of rainwater would assist them with some but not all of their water needs. In time, across the city, structures were built with brick cisterns lined with mortar that were sunk into the ground or with aboveground wooden cisterns for collection of rainwater that poured down on the city sporadically throughout the year.

Dr. Greensville S. Dowell wrote an article in the *Galveston Medical Journal* that stated:

> *All classes use cistern water, principally from brick cisterns, about six feet deep, covered with wood. The well water is brackish and cannot be used for drinking; horses are, however, generally watered at the wells. The brackish water is used for scouring and sometimes for cooking when cistern water is scarce. Yet, even with these cisterns, problems still arose, and something needed to be done regarding the water supply. In response, the city tried its best to crack down by employing the city police department to act as health inspectors and to shut down any unsanitary properties to try to clean up the city.*[11]

Another issue faced by Galveston was the pressure required to force water through the fire hose. Early fire engines required firefighters start to pump a handle to get water into the firebox, and that same pressure was used to push the water through the hose. Later, the pump would be adjusted to use

Left: A wooden cistern behind a home, circa 1908. *Author's collection.*

Below: Two men holding a baby with a wooden cistern behind them, circa 1910. *Author's collection.*

steam to keep it going; however, the pressure was still always low. Due to the low pressure and the bits of shell and sand that clogged their fire nozzles, firefighters found it nearly impossible to put fires out in a timely manner or to get them under control.

In September 1882, a recommendation was placed before the city by the Committee on Water Supply, stating it should engage a hydraulic engineer to find the best way to obtain fresh water. J.D. Cook, a consulting engineer from Toledo, Ohio, was hired to provide recommendations on a saltwater protection system for the city as well as a freshwater system for all uses. Cook investigated several sources of water, and his recommendation was to collect water from reservoirs on the mainland—at Highland Bayou—and pipe it to Galveston Island via a cast-iron pipe or another piping method. Cook strongly urged the city to not seek a saltwater system, since a freshwater system was feasible; he also suggested that a standpipe should be located on the island where the water could be stored. It was on his recommendation that the city eagerly began to solicit bids to have the system constructed.

Shortly after bids were solicited, the Galveston Water Company was formed as a private entity by Morgan Jones, E.P. Woan, H.H. Britton and W.C. Connor to prove a "system of waterworks for the extinguishment of fires, sanitary and other purposes" was a real possibility. An ordinance later passed by the city agreed that the Galveston Water Company was responsible for laying all the necessary pipes and mainlines, erecting hydrants and furnishing water free of charge for city purposes, such as supplying city buildings and park fountains with water and flushing the city streets and gutters. The water company was compensated eight dollars a month by the city for its rental fee of each hydrant. After the waterworks were constructed, the city reserved the right to purchase the hydrants outright.

Eight years later, the city once again looked into a saltwater protection system with 100 hydrants. Construction began on the waterworks on August 10, 1883, and required the completion of the saltwater system by January 1, 1884, and the freshwater system to be completed eighteen months after the contract was signed. The system, when completed, included a pumping station at the foot of Twenty-Sixth Street, near the bay. This station had two sixty-horsepower boilers and two Worthington duplex pumps with a capacity of 2.5 million gallons of water every twenty-four hours. Water was to be drawn from the bay through a sixteen-inch feed pipe and then fed to the system through eight miles of six-inch to twelve-inch pipes that were connected to 110 hydrants throughout the city. City ordinances stated that water pipes would need to be run through the alleys so as not to damage the existing surface of the city streets.

This new system was contained to an area between Seventeenth Street to the east, Thirty-First Street to the west, the bay to the north and Church Street to the south. Contained within this area was most of the business district, the wharves and the cotton compresses.

The original two-story Galveston City Waterworks. *Author's collection.*

To show that it was completed and to be accepted by the City of Galveston, the system would have to have enough pressure to push ten streams of water through one-inch nozzles and a fifty-foot hose to a height of one hundred feet. As the company toiled to complete the system, it dealt with a number of delays that nearly crippled the project; however, the system was completed fifteen days shy of the deadline required for the system.

At about 2:00 p.m. on Tuesday, January 15, 1884, the trial began and continued all throughout the day, with the third and final trial of the day starting at Twenty-Second Street, where the system proved it could indeed live up to its potential, though other tests earlier on were not so impressive. Still, even with the minor issues established with the system, the city did finally accept the hydrant system and declared it met the specifications required by the contract.

A few years later, in 1889, the city continued adding to the water system, with thirteen wells being dug every eight hundred feet along Winnie Street. The system, which cost the city $450,000, consisted of seventeen thousand feet of piping for the water main, a pump house and a standpipe used for fire protection.

During the 1900 hurricane, which decimated over two-thirds of the city, the city waterworks was demolished. Immediately, the city began repairing the system and bringing it back online as quickly as possible. By 1904, a new waterworks had been constructed to replace the building destroyed in the storm.

Over time, the waterworks was expanded along with the growth of the city, and in 1907, meters were installed on all connections to the city waterworks system for the purpose of measuring the water used through the connection. The population of Galveston was consuming nearly 4.5 million gallons of water daily, and in order to meet that need, the Galveston pumping station was going to have to find a way to increase its output. In 1913, the Alta Loma water plant installed new air pumps, which allowed it to pump a supply of 8 million gallons of water to Galveston and its population of nearly forty thousand people daily.

By 1950, a new waterworks had been established at Fifty-Ninth and Strand Streets to work in conjunction with the existing waterworks at Thirtieth Street and Avenue H. New pipes were extended along Broadway

Galveston City Waterworks, damaged by the 1900 storm. *Author's collection.*

Rebuilt one-story Galveston City Waterworks, circa 1904. *Author's collection.*

Street to connect the new station with the existing station and to reach the outer sections of the city. Over time, the City of Galveston laid out more water pipes and hydrants to give the fire department better connections to the water should a fire occur.

Over time, the original saltwater system was discontinued, as it was not as suited for use with a freshwater system.

SEAWALL AND GRADE RAISING

At first, the reader may question how the seawall and grade raising are connected to fire protection; however, it must be understood, these two things protected the city and its citizens, firefighters, fire companies and their equipment. This, in turn, allowed Galveston's fire department to continue to survive and grow with the city.

Galveston was no stranger to hurricanes, which churned the gulf and occasionally visited the island. The earliest known hurricane to strike

Galveston Island made landfall in 1527. Similar storms would follow in 1766 and 1818. The first storm to hit the island after the city was established occurred on October 6, 1837, and it brought a storm tide of six feet, which inundated the city. Joseph Ehlinger suggested rebuilding the destroyed custom house on four-foot pilings to raise it above the flood level. Shortly after that, additional buildings were built on pilings. This practice continued as Galveston began to grow.

Additional storms would follow in 1839, 1842, 1854 and 1867, and they would, once again, inundate the city. Coincidentally, Galveston was struggling through a terrible yellow fever outbreak in 1867, and the city remained flooded for several days, leaving bodies unable to be buried.

In 1886, after a destructive hurricane wiped Indianola, Galveston's rival port city, off the map and filled its harbor, the City of Galveston established a committee to study the topography of the island and suggest ways the city could protect itself from future hurricanes.[12] A seawall was suggested to enclose the city; however, as there was not enough tax revenue and no one believed Galveston would ever be struck by a hurricane of that magnitude, the idea was shelved.

On September 8, 1900, a day that started out like any other, began with weather reports stating conditions would be calm, with little to no rain. As the day progressed, however, that weather prediction would prove to be false. Earlier in the week, many reports had come into the weather station stating that a strong hurricane had crossed Cuba and was headed toward Galveston. Isaac Cline, head of the Galveston Weather Bureau, saw the reports and notified his superiors of the impending storm. Yet he, too, believed that the gulf was too shallow for the creation of a storm that could cause significant damage to the city.

As the summer of 1900 had been one of the hottest on recorded, the citizens of Galveston enjoyed this rain and the cooling winds it produced. Residents and visitors alike still enjoyed the beach, children had bathtub races in the streets and business continued as usual. By midafternoon, the rains picked up; the water became deeper on the streets as the skies darkened. People saw the once ankle-deep water become knee-deep and steadily rise. Galveston's residents and visitors began to realize that this was no regular storm and decided it was time to return to the safety of their lodgings to try to ride this storm out like they had so many others.

Once the storm reached the island city, fear and anxiety skyrocketed. People frantically tried to wade through the waist-deep water to any form of shelter. Winds were hurtling pieces of wood, brick, glass and slate tiles

Above: A view of Indianola, Helmuth Holz, September 1860. *Courtesy of the Library of Congress, LC-93515580.*

Right: Young Isaac Cline. *Courtesy of the National Archives.*

Damage from the 1900 storm. *Author's collection.*

through the air, killing anyone or anything in their path. Galvestonians did what they could to save not only themselves but also their neighbors. As the storm surge hit the island, structures close to the beach were demolished by the tides. This debris, combined with the storm surge, pushed its way into the city, destroying almost everything in its path. For many residents, as the water rose, they used axes to cut holes in the floors of their homes in the hopes of saving them. Structures were crowded with families, neighbors, refugees from the storm and livestock hoping to survive.

Throughout the evening, the winds worsened, water rose and buildings crumbled, taking entire families with them. Eventually, the eye of the storm passed, and a dead calm lay over the city. The water began to recede, and the sun began to rise. At daybreak, survivors of the storm emerged from their shelters to find a landscape foreign to them. What had once been beautiful neighborhoods were then desolate landscapes, void of homes,

Damage from the 1900 storm. *Author's collection.*

discernible landmarks and people. Roads were covered in debris and dead bodies strewn about.

Galveston immediately set to clean up and rebuild itself. The first order of business was to establish the death crews to remove bodies from the island with any carts that were still useable; one such cart to survive was a fire wagon. As the earth was too soaked, it was determined that mass burial was out of the question; so, on Monday, September 10, about seven hundred bodies were loaded onto three barges and towed eighteen miles out into the Gulf of Mexico, where the bodies were buried at sea; however, most of the bodies returned to the island. Finally, it was determined the only way to rid Galveston of its dead was to burn the bodies. Huge funeral pyres were built on the beach and throughout the city, using the debris to burn the bodies.

Once the task of burning the bodies was established, the city focused on rebuilding itself and reestablishing its services. Nearly nine months

A hose cart being used to transport bodies, circa 1900. *Author's collection.*

Building sections of the seawall. *Author's collection.*

The completed seawall. *Author's collection.*

after the 1900 hurricane wrecked the island, a large part of the city of Galveston had already been restored, and it had resumed all of its regular business functions.

Shortly after the storm, it was determined that a seawall was needed to protect the city. The idea of the seawall was not a new or novel one; in fact, it had been discussed at length in the early 1880s but was deemed unnecessary at the time.

With assistance from the State of Texas and local taxes, the city set about building a seawall. Construction began in 1902 at Sixth Street and continued until 1904, when the final section of the seawall was completed at Thirty-Ninth Street. After the seawall was completed, the task of raising Galveston began. The city used this opportunity to not only raise itself but also to deepen the channel in Galveston Bay. Several canals were dug around the city and cofferdams were created around areas that needed to be raised. Residents paid contractors to raise their homes, and the city paid to raise all the city services, including all of the fire hydrants.

After everything was raised, dredge boats pumped silt from the bay, eased into the canals of the city and then pumped the silt into these areas. Once the silt reached the fill line, the water was allowed to drain off. This gargantuan task of raising a city was completed in 1914, having raised over 3,500 buildings.

GALVESTON, TEXAS.
Galveston Grade raising Pumping in the filling.

Opposite, top: Grade raising the canal and a hopper boat, circa 1904. *Author's collection.*

Opposite, middle: A view of the grade raising, showing the raised houses and the silt being pumped in. *Author's collection.*

Opposite, bottom: St. Patrick's Church being raised, circa 1910. *Author's collection.*

Above: A fire plug after the grade raising, Twenty-Fifth at Q½ Streets. *Courtesy of Special Collections, Rosenberg Library, Galveston, Texas.*

FIRE BOATS

With the growth of Galveston's port and the increasing number of cotton and other flammable cargos being shipped, Galveston's long-sensed need for better protection of its port came to the forefront. Galveston handled nearly 4 million bales of cotton, along with other cargos, coming in and out of the city every season. State authorities had long urged the city to purchase a fire tug to protect this valuable cargo as well as the valuable port. It was seen many times where traditional fire apparatuses, such as trucks, were limited in getting to fires located in the wharfs, and trying to fight fires in the holds was even harder.

Galveston's port was bustling, with numerous passenger and cargo ships coming and going on a daily basis. And feeding a busy port were thousands of railcars with hundreds of miles of tracks crisscrossing the many wharves and sheds on the docks. With all of this rail traffic, the ability of the fire department to get to a fire could easily be hampered by a string of cars sitting across the roadway or a train needing to pass by. With the wharf surrounded by railroad lines on one side and water on the other—and with no good way for the fire department to get to a fire—a fire boat was needed.

With a fire tug in the wharf, fires could be fought not only at the wharf but also out at sea. With this in mind, the City of Galveston purchased a deep-sea tugboat for \$35,000 and converted it into a fire boat for another \$17,000. The vessel, originally built in 1899, was over one hundred feet long and capable of throwing four thousand gallons of water a minute from its two-and-a-half-inch revolving nozzle on its forward turret and two-inch revolving nozzle on its aft turret. Aside from being used at the port, the boat could assist with fires on land at a distance of no more than two thousand feet away.

On October 29, 1913, the new fire tug the *Charles Clarke* was placed into service by Chief John H. Gernand of the Galveston Fire Department; it had a crew of ten, with Charles McClusky serving as captain of the vessel. The city established Fire Station No. 9 at Pier 23 to house the vessel and the crew members who would man the ship. The building, a two-story structure, was erected on the northeast corner of Pier 23.

This new vessel was a key piece of firefighting equipment for use on Galveston's busy and thriving port, especially since Galveston handled over 4 million bales of cotton a year, as well as large quantities of cotton seed products. The *Charles Clarke* served the city valiantly from Pier 23 from 1913 to 1928, and then it moved to Pier 22, where it remained from 1928 to

Above. *Charles Clarke*, fire boat. *Courtesy of the Austin Smith Collection.*

Left: Fire Chief John H. Gernand. *Author's collection.*

Top: *City of Galveston*, fire boat. *Courtesy of the Austin Smith Collection.*

Bottom: The *City of Galveston* was called into service, spraying flames at the Texas City Wharf after the disaster on April 16, 1947. *Author's collection.*

1930. In 1928, the city purchased a new fire boat, the *City of Galveston*, for $140,000; two years later, in 1930, the *Charles Clarke* was scrapped.

The *City of Galveston* would serve the Galveston Waterfront from 1930 to 1948, making between two hundred and three hundred calls each year. On April 16, 1947, the *City of Galveston* was called on to assist in the Texas City disaster; however, even with the vessel's distinguished career, in 1949, the city commission chose to discontinue the use of the fire boat due to the cost needed to repair the ship.

Afterward, its fifteen-man crew was reassigned to various stations on the island. Chief William J. Henderson repeatedly requested that repairs, estimated to cost about $35,000, be made to the ship, as, without the ship, the city's wharf was unprotected from fire. For four years, the *City of Galveston*, which was moored in the harbor at Pier 22, in much need of repair, slowly began to rot away. In 1952, the city no longer saw the need for a fire boat, and eventually, the *City of Galveston* was sold for scrap.

3

GALVESTON FIRE DEPARTMENT HISTORY

All cities, whether large or small, have been plagued with the threat of fire and its destruction to city structures. These early cities learned from the very beginning that the organization of a fire prevention company would be in the best interest of the cities themselves and their residents. History recounts numerous "great fires" that destroyed large portions of major urban areas, such as the "Great Fire of New Orleans in 1788" and another in 1794. These early fires prompted Galveston officials to take steps to protect their fledgling city from the threat of fire.

Due to early planning, forethought, early advancements in fire prevention and the major devastation wrought by earlier fires, Galveston's early volunteer company grew to become the very first paid fire department in the state. The humble origins of Galveston's first fire company began on July 23, 1839, when the city's mayor John M. Allen and the city aldermen appointed the first chief engineer and an assistant to organize Engine Company No. 1.

Many of Galveston's earlier structures were made entirely of wood; having been constructed in the North, disassembled, brought to the island and reassembled. One such home, the home of Samuel May Williams, was documented as having been milled and constructed in Maine on the Presumpscot River in the town of Saccarappa and then shipped to Galveston, where it was reassembled.[13] Other early structures in Galveston were usually utilitarian and less grand visually, consisting mainly of wood or other combustible materials.

Samuel May Williams's home, circa 1885. *Courtesy of Special Collections, Rosenberg Library, Galveston, Texas.*

In July 1841, the board of aldermen for the city passed an ordinance that appointed fire wardens for each of the five wards in the city. Each of the wardens was given a large tin shield on which the number of the wearer was stamped. Should a conflagration start, these men were to take charge of the situation and control and direct the efforts of volunteers until the threat was gone.

Early firefighting efforts, though valiant, were meager at best. Should a fire begin, volunteers would be gathered to form a bucket brigade. This bucket brigade consisted of two rows of men, buckets and a water source. One row of men would take the buckets filled with water and pass them along the line to be splashed on the fire. The second group of men would take the empty buckets and pass them along the line to be filled from the nearest water source, so the process could be repeated over and over again until the fire was successfully put out. These early water sources were sometimes cisterns near the structures, the bay, the gulf or even small depressions of land where water gathered from recent rainstorms.

Early efforts to protect the island city were meager, as most structures were of little to no value and their losses did not affect the city. However, as time progressed, more substantial structures began to fill in and take the places of these earlier, insignificant structures, causing a need for a much more efficient and larger fire company. This urgent need led for a call to all citizens of the city to meet and discuss fire safety. On September 30, 1843, Albert Ball, John P. Davie, William Dunbar and Nahor Biggs Yard called the meeting to establish a committee on forming a more permanent firefighting organization. The committee, which included Albert Ball, F.A. Whalley and Jacob L. Briggs, along with the mayor, began to establish a set of bylaws for governing the new proposed fire company.

On October 3, 1843, a second meeting was held, and several men signed on to serve in the newly established fire companies of the city. On December 3, 1843, the new constitution was adopted, Galveston Hook and Ladder Company No. 1 was founded, forty-one volunteers were officially recognized as members of the company and the first piece of equipment purchased was designed by Stephen Kirkland, a blacksmith on Mechanic at Twenty-Second Streets. The city also purchased the first uniforms for the newly appointed fire department, which included red shirts and white belts. On the day the volunteers received their new uniforms, a dinner was held in their honor.

Things seemed to be going well for the early department; however, in 1846, several men from the early fire company decided to break away from the original company and pushed to establish a second company, later known as the Washington Fire Company No. 1. In 1849, the City of Galveston, recognizing the importance of newer equipment and supplies, appropriated money for a brand-new hand-pumped fire engine for the department. The city searched locally for a blacksmith to make the new piece of equipment; however, no local source could be found for such a device. Therefore, Albert Ball commissioned James Smith of New York City to build a modern machine with the most up-to-date features and an ability to throw two good streams of water at the same time.

On January 8, 1850, the newly formed Washington Fire Company No. 1 was organized with fifty-eight members on its roll. While it anticipated the arrival of its new piece of equipment, a committee was organized by the fire company to receive and house a hand engine with the proper ceremonies. In April that year, the committee charged the company with recognizing and renaming itself the Washington Fire Company No. 1. That same year, the newest piece of equipment purchased by the City of Galveston for use by the newly formed fire company arrived in Galveston Harbor from New York aboard the ship the *William B. Travis*. The new hand pump was removed from the ship and stored in a wood shed on Mechanic Street, near Twenty-

Hook & Ladder Company No. 1, 2308 Avenue E, circa 1900. *Author's collection.*

Second Street, directly opposite the old Galveston Daily News Building. In 1857, the city appropriated funds to build a brand-new engine house, where the hand pump was stored until 1875, when a fire destroyed the building.

On March 7, 1856, Island City Fire Company No. 2 was established, and the old hand pump engine that had been used by Washington Fire Company No. 1 was turned over to its care. That same year, a wooden engine house was erected on Mechanic Street, near Seventeenth Street, for use by the company until later in the year. A new cornerstone was laid, and anticipation was high for moving into the new building; however, the contractor took the money and left, leaving the building unfinished and most of his employees unpaid. A new contractor was found, and work continued until the completion of the building in the spring of 1866. That same year, the company was provided with its own steamer from the manufacturing firm of Silsby and Company from New York. This engine was used by the company until a newer first-class engine was given to it for its use in 1871.

On March 7, 1857, Old Axe Company was established with twenty-six members. Each member of the company was issued an axe and put in charge of tearing down wood-frame buildings during fires to stop the spread of the flames. The company did well for many years; however, on the eve of the Civil War, the company was disbanded and never reorganized.

Engine Company No. 2, 1718 Avenue C, circa 1900. *Author's collection.*

Due to a fire in 1869, records were lost on the official formation date of the Star State Company Fire Company No. 3, which was started due to the need for additional fire protection in the city. This company was given a second-class Silsby engine, which it used proudly. Prior to the Civil War, which came to Galveston in 1861, the city's fire department consisted of Hook and Ladder Company No. 1, Island City Fire Company No. 2, Star State Fire Engine Company No. 3 and the Old Axe Company. This group was known as the "Fire Brigade."

In 1860, a group of young men secured an engine from the Galveston, Houston and Henderson Railway Company for their use. This group, known as Young America No. 1, obtained the engine and served a few short years before disbanding.

At the onset of the Civil War, most residents and many business owners left the island and headed to the mainland. Maintaining a fire department was deemed unnecessary; therefore, it was disbanded until after the end of the Civil War. A few men stayed behind to keep an eye on the city and to protect as much of its infrastructure as they could during its occupation and bombardment. At the close of the Civil War, the city was no longer occupied by the Union, and the port was no longer under a blockade. The city's population once again returned, eager to rebuild and return to a semblance of normalcy.

Above: Engine Company No. 3, 2828 Avenue D, circa 1900. *Author's collection.*

Opposite: Engine Company No. 4, 1102 Avenue C, circa 1900. *Author's collection.*

In early 1866, the City of Galveston appropriated $8,000 to the purchase of a newer engine capable of throwing a stream of water one hundred feet into the air. Once again, the firm of Silsby & Company was contracted to manufacture the new hand pump engine. While waiting for the arrival of the new hand pump engine, at a city meeting on May 21, 1866, a resolve was passed that said the new engine would be tested by a group of engineers to prove it was capable of handling what was required of it.

In June 1866, the new steamer arrived from New York on the vessel *Ariadne*. The steamer was tested by a number of engineers, and it performed beautifully. In a little less than two and a half minutes, the steamer was at full capacity, and a stream of water raced through the 50-foot hose and sprayed 179 feet into the air. The engine passed its inspection beautifully and was accepted for use by Washington Fire Company No. 1. The new engine, the first to be put into commission in the state of Texas, drew much attention from various fire companies across the state. Visiting delegates who were looking to purchase a new engine arrived in the city,

and Washington Fire Company No. 1 obliged them by demonstrating its beautiful new hand pump engine.

During this same time, a new company known as Lee Company No. 5, was officially organized on July 8, 1866, and obtained the use of the small engine that had been commissioned by Young America No. 1 for use as its steamer. Lee Company No. 5's headquarters was a small shanty next to the engine house of Island City Fire Company No. 2. This served as the company's headquarters until June 1867, when it was reorganized as Lee Fire Company No. 5 and became a regular member of the fire department. It also obtained the original engine used by the Star State Fire Company No. 3; the company used the engine until 1874, when the Galveston Board of Aldermen purchased a brand-new steamer.

On December 12, 1866, the City of Galveston once again reestablished the volunteer fire company. On April 21, 1868, a new hand pump engine company known as Beauregard No. 4 came into existence. It obtained a brick firehouse on Seventeenth Street, between Market and Mechanic Streets. That same year, on May 2, 1868, a meeting was held by a group

Above: Hose Company No. 5, 1614 Avenue K, circa 1900. *Author's collection.*

Opposite: Hose Company No. 6, 3716 Avenue J, circa 1900. *Author's collection.*

of young men to take charge of one of the older pump engines. Twenty-six men enrolled, and the name Mechanics No. 6 was chosen. The company's first headquarters was located at the intersection of Tremont and Winnie Streets, and it remained there for a number of years. After several years of service, the company was supplied with a new steam engine

On June 6, 1869, Beauregard No. 4 failed and was dissolved as a company. Shortly after the loss of Beauregard No. 4, a new company, Hope Fire Company No. 4, arose in its place and took over the duties of its predecessor. All seemed to be going well for the new company until October 1870, when, for some unknown reason, the city's board of aldermen passed an ordinance allowing for the sale of the horses used to pull the engines. The exasperated volunteers marched with their wagon to the Central Market, where they handed over the engine to the city.

In the winter of 1869, another company, the Young Eagles, was established, and on January 7, 1870, a new title, Eagles No. 7, was chosen. The company was in existence for only a few short years before it disbanded.

Above: Hose Company No. 7, 3714 Avenue P, circa 1900. *Author's collection.*

Opposite: Firefighter parade at Postoffice Street and Twenty-Third Street, circa 1872. *Courtesy of the Austin Smith Collection.*

On April 21, 1870, Washington Fire Company No. 1 paraded seventy-four members strong with its engine, draped with a banner that stated, "The People's Friend"; it was covered in flowers and held a portrait of George Washington. After Hope Company relinquished its engine to the city, a new company stepped forward to lay claim to it; this company, known as Protection Fire Company No. 8, was organized on October 30, 1870. The men were given charge of the engine as well as the engine house and became valuable members of the early department.

On December 2, 1870, the Phoenix Hook and Ladder Company No. 2 was established along with a truck house at Market Street on Twenty-Fifth Street, then known as Bath Avenue. A short time later, a brand-new engine was procured by Chief Engineer Frank Hitchcock, which arrived in Galveston and was placed into the care of the company.[14]

Sadly, while Chief Engineer Hitchcock was returning from New York on the *Veruna* after procuring the engine, the ship foundered at sea, and all the passengers were lost. With the loss of the *Veruna*, the city also lost Chief Engineer Hitchcock.

Undeterred, the men of Hope Company gained subscriptions from their friends and family and raised enough money to obtain their own engine from the City of Mobile, Alabama; they later secured a charter, on May 6, 1871, from the State of Texas to start their own company. A short time later, the company was granted the right to join the local fire department. Later on, the name of the company was changed to Hope No. 5.

On May 26, 1873, a request for a paid fire department was brought forth by Alderman Ferdinand Mosebach, who stated that "no more fire or hook and ladder companies [should] be accepted or commissioned, with a view of organizing a paid department....All pay to volunteer companies, except feed for horses, drivers' wages and other necessary expenses, be... hereby abrogated, [and] after the expiration of the present year the chief of the fire department shall receive no pay for his services whatsoever."[15] Thankfully, most of this request never came to fruition, and the volunteers retained their duties.

Henry Rosenberg. *Author's collection.*

In 1876, two members of the volunteer company were brought up on charges of arson, leading the city to contemplate a paid department once again. This act forced the city aldermen to amend the ordinance to ensure stricter regulations and the ability to remove a member from the force in the case of misconduct.

In 1882, the final early company to be organized was Western Fire Company No. 6, the successor of Mechanics No. 6. While the volunteer companies fought bravely to protect the city from the dangers of fire, it was noted that many volunteers were scattered throughout the city, thus slowing the response time of the departments to threats of fire. And with the city's continued growth and expansion, the need for a paid department was becoming much more apparent. These talks of establishing a paid department had been brought to the forefront by the local papers, which suggested firefighting should be placed in the hands of those who would give it their utmost attention. The earliest of these discussions began in 1873; many times, they even suggested creating a paid department. In the summer of 1885, the city leaders organized a committee to look into the feasibility of creating a paid fire department.

The committee consisted of Henry Rosenberg, Julius Runge, Fenlon Cannon, Francis W. Lammers and James McDonald. A majority of the committee members, including Rosenberg, Runge, Cannon and Lammers, presented a report that favored the adoption of a paid fire department and the dissolution of the volunteer departments. This resolution was drafted on September 21, 1885; it dissolved the unpaid volunteer companies and created a paid company. The resolution read on September 23, 1885, was passed with a unanimous vote.

With the passing of the ordinance, Alderman Albert Weis issued a resolution that stated:

> *Whereas, the Volunteer Fire Department of the City of Galveston for nearly a half century have kept guard and vigil over the houses and property of our own people against the ravages of fire, without other reward than the gratitude of the public and the consciousness of duty performed.*

> *Whereas, being composed of men of intelligence, civic virtue and moral worth, they have always responded with alacrity and zeal to every call for succor to the extent of imperiling their lives for the good of the fellow citizens; and*
>
> *Whereas, the city has progressed in populating and general prosperity to a point when the brave men who have so long borne the brunt of battle without fee or reward deserve an honorable retirement from their hazardous and perilous duties; and,*
>
> *Whereas, the city has deemed it a just tribute to brave and self-sacrificing men to pay for services so arduous and well appreciated by the reorganization of the department under a paid system; therefore, be it resolved, that in parting with the old guard of fire heroes of the city council, on behalf of a generous public, members, with pride in their long service, the heroic devotion to duty and their unwavering loyalty to law, order and good-citizenship, and wishes for them in the future, health, honor, peace and prosperity.*[16]

Two days later, the board of aldermen met for the select purpose of choosing a chief engineer. Three men's names were added to the list of nominations for the position: Martin Davey, John Cotter and William Oldenburg. From the nominations, William Oldenburg was chosen, as he had already been acting as chief of the volunteer fire department. That day, several men were chosen to fill the newly created paid positions of the department.

Prior to the establishment of the paid fire department, firehouses were located on properties large enough to store equipment and house horses; however, they were not owned by the city. Therefore, it was determined much more suitable permanent structures would be provided for the newly created department. In the beginning, three stations were established. Fire Station 1, or Central Fire Station, was established on Postoffice Street, between Twenty-Third and Twenty-Fourth Streets. Fire Station No. 2 was located on Mechanic Street, between Seventeenth and Eighteenth Streets. And Fire Station No. 3 was located on Church Street, between Twenty-Fifth and Twenty-Sixth Streets.

Since that time, the fire department has undergone a number of changes—changes that have included newer, more-up-to-date stations and equipment, additional positions and newly created sections within the fire department itself.

By 1950, the Galveston Fire Department had eleven fire stations within the city limits, which ended at Sixty-First Street. In 1961, after Hurricane

Left: Central Fire Station, circa 1914. *Courtesy of the Austin Smith Collection.*

Below: Galveston City Hall and city auditorium, circa 1918. *Author's collection.*

Carla came through Galveston and left a wake of destruction, it was determined that a new Central Fire Station should be built. Due to the massive damage done to the city auditorium, a decision was made to demolish the auditorium, and the new station was built on the site. By 1965, Fire Station No. 1, also known as Central Fire Station No. 1, was relocated to 2514 Sealy Street, behind Galveston's City Hall.

By 1968, the fire department was listed as having only six fire stations, as many had been closed, renumbered or relocated. Due to a large brush fire in 1976, the same year that the Jamaica Beach Volunteer Fire Department

Central Fire Station, 1961–2020. It was originally site of the city auditorium. *Author's collection.*

Central Fire Station, circa 2020. *Author's collection.*

was established, a fire station, No. 7, was built at near 12 Mile Road. Sea Isle obtained its fire station, Fire Station No. 8, in 1989.

In 2008, with the destructive winds and water from Hurricane Harvey, the city lost two fire stations that were rebuilt at their current locations. Since that time, new stations have been built around the city. In 2016, the City Office of Emergency Management was placed under the direction of the Galveston Fire Department. Just recently, the City of Galveston built a new Central Fire Station on Sealy Street, behind the Moody Mansion, which replaced the 1961 Central Fire Station.

Today's current fire department consists of four divisions: fire administration, prevention, operations and special operations. It currently operates six engine companies and two ladder trucks from six fire stations with two battalion chiefs.

4
THE DISTRICT FIRES

The threat of fire has been a continuous plague to the city of Galveston from its very founding. However, even with the numerous fires that have occurred on the island, source documentation is limited. In this chapter, the goal is to share the stories of the island's most disastrous fires in terms of monetary damage to property or loss of life.

This chapter, which lists numerous fires, is in no way a complete list. In this chapter, Galveston has been broken into four districts: the commercial district, the residential district, the wharf district and the warehouse district. Please see the accompanying map to determine the boundaries of these districts.

The commercial district section discusses the area that includes the major business hub of the city. The residential district section covers all areas of the island that contain the homes of the island city's residents; this area includes the East End, Lost Bayou, Silk Stocking, Kempner Park Area, et cetera. The wharf district section focuses solely on the Port of Galveston and the many wharfs and buildings that are located in this area. The warehouse district section focuses on the area of Galveston roughly bounded between Harborside and Broadway Streets, between Thirty-Seventh Street and Fifty-Ninth Street.

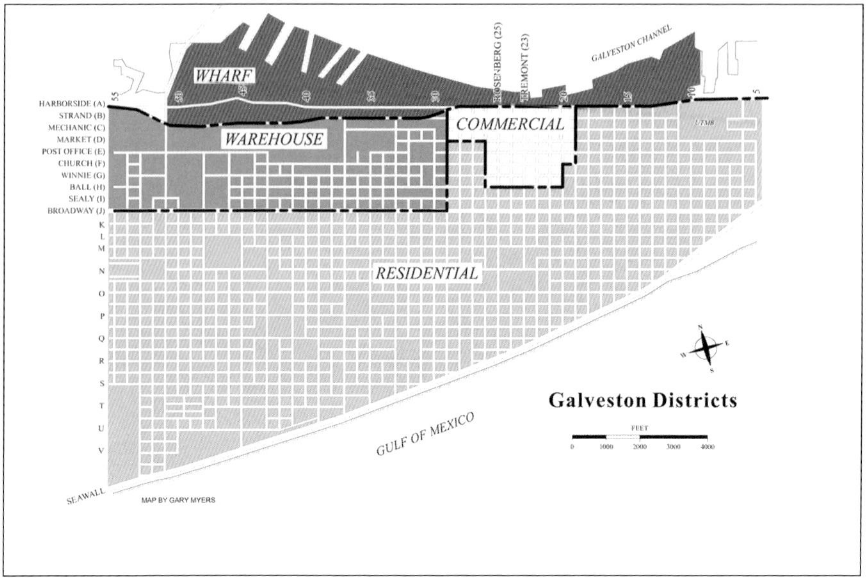

City of Galveston District Map, created by Gary Meyers for the author. *Courtesy of Gary Meyers.*

COMMERCIAL DISTRICT

August 2, 1865
The Corner of Market and Tremont Streets

Around midnight, a fire began on Tremont Street, destroying a row of wooden buildings on the corner of Market and Tremont Streets at an estimated cost of $15,000. Three of the four buildings on the corner opposite the old Commercial and Agricultural Bank belonged to Mr. Henri de St. Cyr. While the other building on the alley belonged to a Mr. Conn. Charles H. Leonard, Esq., the mayor of the city, occupied the building on the corner of Tremont and Market Streets, and the adjoining building belonged to Mr. Philip Dubie.

Upon further inspection, it was found that these buildings had been broken into, and items had been taken. It seems the fire originated in Mr. Conn's building and progressed to the saloons that were occupied by Mayor Leonard and Mr. Dubie. In each case, the buildings were found to have been broken into, and in the case of the saloons, all of the liquor had been taken. Thankfully, some of the furniture was able to be saved from the fire.

Several buildings in the area began catching fire, like the wood cornice and shed of Mr. Sauter's four-story brick building on the opposite side of Tremont Street. The Columbia Hotel on Strand Street caught fire as well as the Buckley and Byrnes Buildings. Thankfully, the firemen were able to put out these fires; however, the four buildings where the fire began were already smoldering ruins due to their dry nature. It is believed that these fires were set intentionally; however, finding the culprit was hard, as the fires were set from different points.

Other buildings that were broken into and set on fire around this time were the old post office building on the corner of Market Street and Twenty-Second Streets, Mr. Sergeant's building on Market Street, Mr. George W. Beissner's building near the Market Street and Mr. Gerald Van Benthuysen's and Mr. James P. Sherwood's building. It was also found that the building owned by Mr. Ernest H. Seiling on Market Street had been broken into and robbed.

According to City Marshal John H. Westerlage, attempts were made to burn the city prior to the departure of U.S. troops from the city. The marshal and several guards were on alert all night, watching the city; though it was impossible for them to guard everything.

View looking up Strand Street from Twentieth Street, 1861. Shown in this picture is the Moro Castle, which would later burn on December 3, 1869. *Courtesy of Special Collections, Rosenberg Library, Galveston, Texas.*

Evans and Company Grocers
December 9, 1866
Twenty-First Street, near Strand Street

On the night of December 9, 1866, flames were found leaping from the three-story Hendley Building at the corner of Twenty-First and Strand Streets. The building had been built by brothers William and Joseph Hendley and was occupied by Evans and Company Grocers, which had been founded in 1856 by William Evans. The fire alarm broke the stillness of the night, and fire companies rushed to get the flames out. Sparks and pieces of wood were flying from the burning building in all directions, threatening to destroy the other buildings in the vicinity. Several roofs were burned by the debris, including the Odd Fellows Hall and the bulletin office. By the time the flames were brought under control, the damage to the building and the loss of its contents were estimated to be about $80,000.

Hendley Building, HABS, circa the 1930s. *Courtesy of the Library of Congress, HABS TEX,84-GALV,37.*

Well before the fire, it was noted the front and back doors to the building had been left wide open, allowing access to anyone who dared to enter the building. During the blaze, business owners began preparing to move their goods from the buildings should fire threaten them. Also, looting became a major threat, as people dashed into the buildings, trying to take goods.

Chapman and Duffield Fire
December 17, 1866
Corner of Tremont and Postoffice Streets

On December 17, nearly two weeks after a fire had nearly destroyed Evans and Company Grocers, a fire decimated the Hendley Building on Strand Street. Another fire was found to have originated at the corner of Tremont and Postoffice Streets in the new building occupied by J.H.F. Chapman & J.J. Duffield. The flames had already started to consume the building and began spreading to buildings nearby. Many of the other adjoining buildings were damaged in the blaze, as was a portion of the Masonic hall. When the fire was finally put out, the damage to the buildings and the contents cost about $30,000.

October 24, 1869
Corner of Market and Tremont Streets

On October 24, 1869, around 1:00 a.m., a major fire broke out in a row of wooden buildings that occupied the corner of Market and Tremont Streets. The fire ravaged and consumed all that was in its path, and before it was contained, it consumed five buildings that contained the cigar store owned by August Bader on Tremont Street and the counting rooms of the *Galveston Daily News* owned by Willard Richardson.

While the loss of the buildings only cost about $15,000, the contents of the buildings caused the loss to total $50,000. Surprisingly, even with the fire, the *Galveston Daily News* was still able to deliver its morning edition; however, the new German paper that had been scheduled to come out that day didn't fare so well.

Moro Castle Fire
December 3, 1869
Corner Tremont and Strand Streets

Around 1:20 a.m. on the morning of Friday, December 3, 1869, a watchman who was making his rounds noticed smoke emanating from the Moro Castle, a three-story wooden structure on the corner of Tremont and Strand Streets. Moro Castle was built by Philp Moro in the late 1830s on Galveston's Strand. The building, a fine Greek Revival wood structure, housed the clothing store of the Cohen Brothers and was completely consumed in the blaze. Five minutes after the alarm was pulled, no engines had yet reached the blaze. Spectators reported seeing flames pouring from unopened doors and windows. A consensus on the origin of the fire said that it appeared to be incendiary in nature and had most likely begun under the staircase leading to the second floor. The entirety of the Cohen Brothers' establishment was consumed in the blaze, and an exceedingly high wind

Ruins after the destructive Moro Castle fire, photographed by Joseph M. Maurer. *Courtesy of Special Collections, Rosenberg Library, Galveston, Texas.*

More of the ruins in the commercial district after the destructive Moro Castle fire, photographed by Joseph M. Maurer. *Courtesy of Special Collections, Rosenberg Library, Galveston, Texas.*

from the northwest whipped up the flames, spreading them further. From the epicenter of the fire, flames spread in all directions; however, they followed a somewhat southern direction, destroying the blocks between Strand and Postoffice Streets and between Mechanic and Church Streets.

As the flames continued to spread down Strand Street, they consumed the buildings that housed Jalonick and Smith, door and sash dealers managed by Isaac Jalonick & J.F. Smith; Henry Runge; Albert Ball Clothing; J.F. Magale's liquor store; Craig & Ruff, dealers in liquors; Lynch and Company; Shields and Company; the new Merchant's Mutual Insurance Company; a saloon owned by Martin Davey; and a clothing store owned by Denis Neils. As the flames spread down Tremont Street, the jewelry firm of Michael W. Shaw and Company; Reinecke and Company, dealers in fine cigars; Rice and Baulard, paint and oiler dealers; Robinson and Company, book merchants; the Palmetto House; and Stauffacher's Sunny South saloon were consumed. As the fire crossed Mechanic Street, the theater caught fire, which sent flames to the firm of A.T. Vanzille, Mr. Brete and Mr. Philip Dubie. Joseph Labadie's gun and ammunition business was damaged by the fire, though thankfully, the gunpowder had been removed. From there, the fire crossed Twenty-Fourth Street and began consuming the store of John G. Rost and Company, a saloon owned by W. Worzlow and Willard Richardson's home before finally being extinguished.

Through divine intervention, several stores were spared from the flames. Dennis Weil's residence and an unoccupied building on Mechanic Street were saved from the blaze. In total, there were about fifty businesses and shopkeepers that were burned out by the start of business that day. The loss was estimated to cost anywhere from $1 million to $1.5 million.

February 24, 1870
Strand Street, Between Twenty-Second and Twenty-Third Streets

On February 24, 1870, a fire broke out in a row of buildings on Strand Street, between Twenty-Second and Twenty-Third Streets. While the exact point of origin was uncertain, it was determined that the fire began on the north side of Strand Street in a row of buildings and then later crossed the street and began consuming buildings on the south side of the street.

After the fire had consumed the lot and had been extinguished, the loss was then estimated to cost over $100,000. The buildings that had been lost to the fire belonged to Albert Ball. The occupants of the building included Judge Edward T. Austin, William H. and John S. Seller; Union Fire and Insurance Company; and Rogers and Company.

Adjoining the Ball Building was a building owned by Mr. Alexander Edgar that was occupied by George Grover and Company, grocers. Continuing down the block, the Sergeant Building, occupied by Levy and Company, dealers in tobacco products and J.C. Gorham, which dealt in carriages and buggies, was reduced to rubble, and after the fire, it was determined that damage cost about $1 million.

Hitchcock and Company
December 19, 1872
Twenty-First Street, at Strand Street

On December 19, 1872, at about 7:30 p.m., smoke was seen coming from the shed at the back of the ship chandlery store of J.F. Hitchcock and Company. The shed, large in size, was used to store tar used by the chandlery store. When the fire was found, the alarm was quickly sounded, and the fire department quickly made its way to the fire. As the trucks arrived on scene, streams of water from hoses along the Central and Brick Wharves were led to the buildings that were on fire. Due to a brisk northerly wind, the flames were fanned, and they continued to commute to nearby buildings, enveloping them in flame as well. The flames continued down the block and licked at the brick buildings opposite as the firemen continued to fight the blaze. Thankfully, the brick buildings were saved; however, the buildings, which were once owned by the Thomas M. League, estate were totally damaged. Thankfully, they were insured for $2,500.

After the fire was out, it was found that a number of businesses had lost a considerable amount, though it was hard to calculate the exact cost. Businesses such as Hitchcock and Company Ship Chandlery had a large amount of stock in their stores, partially covered by a $27,000 insurance plan. James Day and Company, dealers in hay, corn and oats, had lost nearly $800 in stock; however, it had no insurance to cover the cost. Robert Miller, a butcher who had an office in Hitchcock's store, lost all of his office furniture. James McDonald, a dealer in tobacco, saved much of his stock; however, he had no insurance coverage. Other businesses located near the fire contained the damage to their buildings but did not receive any

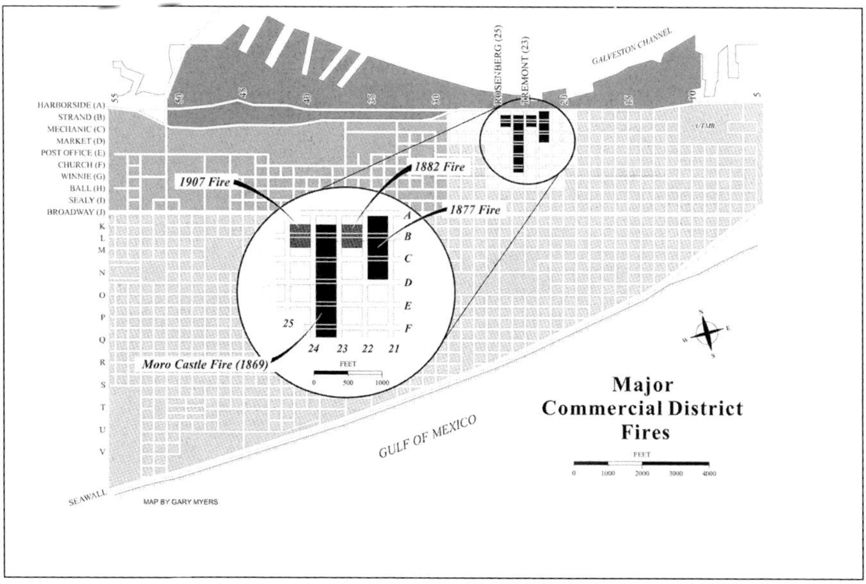

Major Commercial District Fires Map. *Courtesy of Gary Meyers.*

damage to their books or stock. The wholesale grocers of Louis LeGierse and Henry Schulte received considerable damage to their stock due to the water sprayed on the brick buildings owned by Henry Rosenberg and Ebenezer B. Nichols.

As the fire was investigated, it was determined that it was more than likely of an incendiary origin, as the shed where the fire began was quite a ways from the shop itself and no fire source was kept in or near the building. After the fire, the safes of Hitchcock and Company, which were saved from the fire, were returned to their owners.

April 3, 1873
Strand Street

On the night of Thursday, April 3, a fire was discovered on Strand Street, between Center and Twenty-Second Streets, which caused considerable damage to the businesses of Collett and Davis, William Windmeyer, J.W. Wicks, James Sorely and Mr. Gonzales. The total loss of the blaze was roughly $50,000, although the buildings were fully insured.

J.G. Rost and Company Grocers
March 2, 1875
Mechanic Street at Twenty-Fourth Street

Around 3:00 a.m. on March 2, 1875, a fire was discovered in the rear of a building owned by Charles H. Jordan and occupied by grocer and ship chandlers J.G. Rost and Company. Early on, flames were seen making their way through the building. Flames were seen in the southeast windows on the lower windows and the northwest windows on the second story. An alarm was sounded, and within moments, the fire department was on site, doing all it could to put out the flames. Due to the combustible materials used in the building's construction, the entire structure and all of its contents were lost in the flames and smoke. The loss of the building cost $100,000.

Southwick Building
April 23, 1876
Strand Street at Twenty-Fourth Street

The fire began in the Southwick Building, built by Steven Southwick and located at the corner of Strand and Twenty-Fourth Streets. The flames spread to the adjoining frame buildings and continued to burn. By the time the fire was put out, the loss was estimated to cost $100,000.

Dargan and Tobyn Building
August 1, 1876
Corner of Strand and Tremont Streets

An alarm was received around 2:30 a.m. from box 5 at the corner of Twenty-Second and Strand Streets from the building owned by Philip Dargan and David Tobyn. The fire started in a room on the third floor, next to the United States Signal Office.

The room in which the fire was discovered was found to have been used as a storeroom for furniture and household goods that belonged to Mr. Dargan. The fire was found to have started between the floors at the site of a rat's nest. It was thought the fire was started by a rat with some sort of match or flammable material.

When the fire department arrived at the scene, Mr. Oliver H. Bassett, a member of Protection No. 8, climbed the ladder and was near the top when the weight of several men caused the ladder to buckle and Mr. Bassett to fall fifty feet, spinning in the air to the ground below. Shortly after the fall, Mr. Bassett was taken to the hospital and recuperated, though he was unable to return to work for several months. When he did return, his face was partially paralyzed due to the fall. Mr. Bassett returned to work as a highly active member of Hose Company No. 6.

The fire was quickly put out with little to no damage to the building, except for a small, oblong hole that was burned through the floor. The fire was smothered by mattresses that were piled on the floor.

Business District
Strand, Mechanic and Market Streets
June 9, 1877

At 3:30 a.m., the most destructive fire to hit Galveston occurred in the busy commercial district. The fire alarm rang from box 5 as the fire department raced to the scene. The fire started at the New York restaurant owned by Frank Gardoni and continued consuming additional buildings in its path. The flames were spreading to the right and left as the fire moved north toward the harbor, over many more wood-frame buildings, throwing flames and cinders as it progressed. The flames engulfed the Island City Savings Bank and the east side of the street, consuming the Bird Cage Saloon as well as the millinery shops of Mrs. Sam Dixon and Mrs. Paul Knoll.

Next, the fire set its sights toward the Grand Southern Hotel on the corner of Mechanic and Twenty-Second Streets, which it consumed within twenty minutes. Upon arrival, the firemen courageously fought to throw streams of water on the blaze to bring it under control; however, the flames

Destruction from the June 9, 1877 fire. *Courtesy of Special Collections, Rosenberg Library, Galveston, Texas.*

Old Washington Hotel, located at Twenty-First and Mechanic Streets. *Courtesy of Special Collections, Rosenberg Library, Galveston, Texas.*

continued to spread even further, devouring more of the great commercial district of Galveston. Buildings such as the Seeligson and Company Bank on Twenty-Second Street between Strand and Mechanic Streets was devoured as well as a building that was once used as an addition to the Old Washington Hotel on the corner of Twentieth and Mechanic Streets. These buildings were victim to the flames, as the fire seemed hell-bent on destroying the city.

The fire moved swiftly across nearly three blocks, devouring twenty-six buildings as it sought to quench its hunger. Structures such as the Engine House for Washington Fire Company No. 1 and Hook and Ladder Company No. 1 on Mechanic Street were lost as the flames continued its path. On Strand, the fire consumed the James Sorely Building, the Marx and Harris Kempner Building and the Leon and H. Blum Building. Also lost in the blaze was the Brown and Lang building that was built by James Moreau Brown and Clara Lang and housed the J.S. Brown Hardware Company.[17]

When all was said and done, three blocks of the commercial district lay in ashes. Twenty-six buildings, large and small, were lost to the flames. Once-grand buildings had been reduced to rubble, and their fine contents had been reduced to ashes. The cost of the damages soared upward of $300,000.

Jemison, Groce and Company
January 13, 1882
Strand Street, Between Twenty-Second and Twenty-Third Streets

Between 1:00 pm and 2:00 pm, a fire broke out in the cotton sample rooms of the Jemison, Groce and Company, owned by Elbert S. Jemison and William L. Moody. The rooms were located in the rear of the Moody Building on the corner of Strand and Twenty-Second Streets. Reports stated that it seemed as if some cotton samples had caught on fire in the room, and a young boy was the first to report the fire. Upon the call of fire, many folks raced to the room to try to extinguish the flames; however, the flames were not to be contained. The fire grew and continued to consume the entire Moody Building. Several businesses had offices in the building; however, the most devastating loss came to the supreme court and the court of appeals, which were located on the third floor of the building.

The entire floor was damaged; judges' offices and libraries were lost, along with many court records. Within a brief time, the flames began to work their way through the warehouse building of the Greenleve, Block and Company, which was on the adjoining corner. Quickly, the flames moved up the block, seemingly unchecked, with aid from the strong winds that continued to push it forward like a hungry demon. The walls of the Moody Building began to crash down, as did the front wall of the Greenleve, Block and Company.[18]

The firemen fought the flames valiantly and used all their resources against this frightful conflagration that was engulfing the busy commercial district. Just when it seemed the flames would destroy much more of the city, the flames began to subside and brought into check. The fire was completely brought under control at the Brown Hardware Store, run by John S. Brown. The estimated losses from the fire cost more than $700,000.

Shortly after this fire, William L. Moody hired Nicholas J. Clayton to design a new building that was to be built in place of the fire-damaged building.

The second building designed by Nicholas Clayton to replace the original building, which burned circa 1880. *Author's collection.*

Tremont Hotel
May 3, 1885
Corner of Twenty-Third and Church Streets

At 7:30 a.m. on Sunday, May 3, 1885, one of the great boilers of the Tremont Hotel exploded, instantly killing a number of people and wounding several others. Those killed in the explosion were several children of Lawrence Carr, Clara Mill and Anderson Jones. Aside from those killed, several hotel employees, including Jose Aquillo, the pastry cook, were badly bruised and injured; Maurice Sullivan had his collarbone broken and was badly cut all over his head. Mrs. Burns, the linen woman, had her head bruised; R. Walton, the waiter, had his arm broken and received several bruises; and Jon Axman, the bellboy, had his shoulder broken.

Since the boiler was faulty, it exploded, shaking the hotel violently and destroying the little brick building that housed it on the northwest corner of

The second Tremont Hotel, which stood on the corner of Twenty-Third and Church Streets. *Author's collection.*

the hotel. The northwest wing of the hotel was severely damaged, and the boiler was sent hurtling through the air and across Twenty-Fourth Street, where it passed through a two-story servants' quarters. The boiler continued its trajectory and landed in a house of ill repute, nearly destroying the structure and leaving not one stick still standing.

Moore, McKinney and Company
April 19, 1892
Mechanic Street, at Twenty-Fourth Street

On Tuesday, the large grocery firm of Moore, McKinney and Company, jointly owned by James Moore, Liberty S. McKinney and Max Maas and situated in the George Seeligson Building, narrowly escaped being destroyed by a fire that was started on the second floor of the establishment. By the time the flames were discovered, the building was completely consumed by smoke.

The fire department responded quickly to the call, and due to its diligent work, the flames were extinguished and the block was saved from being completely destroyed. James Moore examined the building and found the stock on the first and second floors completely soaked with water. While the official cause of the fire was yet to be determined, James Moore thought that the fire had started when a cigarette or match had been carelessly tossed aside. A conservative estimate said the damage to the building and its contents cost about $80,000.

Oppenheimer and Company
December 2, 1893
Market Street, Between Twenty-Fourth and Twenty-Fifth Streets

At about 12:30 p.m. on Sunday, December 2, 1869, a fire broke out on the third floor of the Kaufman, Leopold Oppenheimer and Company Furniture Store between Twenty-Fourth and Twenty-Fifth Streets on the north side of Market Street. At the onset of the blaze, the person who reported the fire ran directly to Engine House No. 1; it wasn't until several moments later that a general alarm was sent out from box 31 to notify the rest of the fire department of the flames. The fire department responded quickly to the blaze and began putting streams of water on the fire in hopes of extinguishing the quickly growing fire.

The fire originated in the workshop and repair shop on the third floor of the building at the front eastern corner. Quickly, ladders were raised against the building, and hoses were hoisted through the front and back windows so that streams of water could be put on the blaze. Due to the quick and effective work done by the fire department, the blaze was brought under control and kept to the third floor, though the water that was used to put out the blaze and the smoke from the blaze did damage goods on the first and second floors.

Mr. Oppenheimer had been on the second floor of the building, showing a guest goods, when smoke was noted coming from the ceiling area, close to where the workshop was located. Although there was a stove in the area for heating glue, it was believed this was not the origin of the blaze, as it had not been lit since Monday. It was thought that a cigarette or an ember may have been dropped by a workman.

After an hour on the scene, the fire department had put the blaze out; however, several firefighters were injured when a ladder broke and sent them crashing to the roof of the building below. Three firefighters were on the ladder when it broke, but only two were injured and they were quickly removed from the scene, examined and treated. The other fireman was able to grab hold of the lower half of the broken ladder and climb down to safety.

Mr. Oppenheimer stated that he cared deeply for those affected by the fire and the firemen and that he wanted any of their bills sent directly to him. After the fire, the damage to the building and stock was estimated to cost $30,000.

April 6, 1907
Strand Street, Between Twenty-Fourth and Twenty-Fifth Streets

Around 1:35 p.m. on Saturday afternoon, a fire erupted from the back of a brick building on the Strand Street, between Twenty-Fourth and Twenty-Fifth Streets. The flames came from a business that sold secondhand furniture. It seems that the conflagration originated from a gasoline flame beneath a glue pot. The first alarm was sounded by Mr. John Sgiteovich, a bookkeeper for his brother George at 2406 Sealy Street. The flames originated in the furniture store of Mrs. Leaman, who called it to the attention of Mr. Sgiteovich.

Upon entering the store, Sgiteovich saw the shop in flames and ran to the nearest fire alarm box to call the fire department to the scene. While Sgiteovich searched for the key to the box, another witness to the flames called the fire department, which hurried to the scene. Within minutes, a stream of water was put on the front of the building to control the flames. Meanwhile, as other apparatuses arrived, additional streams were put on the building from all sides. Although the streams were steady, the pressure of the streams was very weak.

As if the flames were not bad enough, a dense smoke began to billow from the furniture store, where a number of flammable materials were stored. Due to the thick smoke, the firemen were unable to see the fire and could only guess the direction in which to aim the spray. At the rear of the Hutchings Building, the flames were bursting from the windows and making rapid

The Sealy Building on Strand Street consumed by fire. *Author's collection.*

Debris on the corner of Strand and Rosenberg Streets from the Sealy building fire. *Courtesy of the Galveston County Museum.*

headway through the building. Due to a strong wind, the flames got ahead of the firemen and continued to threaten the buildings around it. Thankfully, the Galveston Shoe and Hat Factory was saved from the flames, as was the Focke, Wilkens and Lange Wholesale Grocery across the alley from the fire.

An explosion in the first section of the Hutchings Building caused the flames to continue to spread and caused the rear wall of the building to crash into the alley below. The fire began to encroach on the Sealy Building next door, which housed several offices of the Santa Fe Railroad. The auditors in their offices tried to save their files and furniture when flames appeared from the ceiling and began to burn their way through the building. Due to the decorative copper used in the ceiling of the offices, the flames took on a bright blue hue. Eventually, all efforts to save records were abandoned, and everyone rushed from the offices to safety.

With the building entirely in flame, burning embers and papers floated from the building into the air and landed far from their source; it was soon realized that the fire was not going to be contained. It was at time that others began to notice how close the burning papers and flames were beginning to drift to the storage headquarters of the Waters Pierce Old Company and the Union Station.

At 4:05 p.m., the rear walls of the Sealy Building collapsed, and the firemen began to focus on trying to stop the flames instead of trying to protect the surrounding property. It was at an extremely late hour in the evening that the flames were finally arrested. Due to the destruction of the fire, many pillars of brick stood precariously above the streets. Therefore, it was determined that they needed to be pulled down to keep them from collapsing.

Sadly, due to the fire, Galveston lost the Sealy Building owned by John Sealy and Waverly R. Smith. This building had originally been built by Nicholas Clayton for the Gulf Colorado and Santa Fe Railway and had been used for the last several years by the Santa Fe Railroad for its auditing department. Also lost were the John Henry Hutchings Building and the Pritchard O'Rourke Building. With the destruction of these buildings, Galvestonians also saw the loss of several rooms that had been outfitted for the use of the Jewish Immigration Bureau as temporary quarters for Jewish immigrants arriving in Galveston.

The saddest loss from this fire came to Mr. William Wallace Patch and his sister, who owned a curio and shell shop in the building. As they had been advancing in age, they were in the middle of selling all of their goods and retiring. However, due to the fire, they both lost all of their possessions and their stock, leaving them penniless.

O.K. Laundry, Direct Navigation Company, Armour Meat Packing Plant 1915 Hurricane August 17, 1915

With the advancing storm, the breaking of the fire alarm system and high water, the city of Galveston suffered a number of fires.

At 8:00 p.m. on Monday, at Twentieth and Postoffice Streets, the O.K. Laundry caught fire. An alarm was sounded, and the fire department dashed into the high water and high winds to try to save the building. As the horses would not budge, a hose was rushed out into the water and raced to the scene; however, hard as they tried, the firefighters were unable to control the blaze, and they watched as the fire burned out. The estimated cost of the fire was $100,000.

Later that evening, around about 9:00 p.m., a fire broke out on the waterfront. The winds were raging at seventy-four miles an hour when the alarm was sounded, and the two-story structure was completely engulfed. The fire was about one and a half blocks away from the Galveston Daily News building and was even closer to the cotton exchange; however, thankfully, the fire burned itself out before consuming anything else. The estimated loss cost $2,000.

The burned ruins of the O.K. Laundry at 414–18 Twentieth Street the day after the 1915 hurricane struck Galveston. *Courtesy of the Galveston County Museum.*

A horse-drawn steam pump in use on the flooded Strand Street during the 1915 hurricane. *Courtesy of the Galveston County Museum.*

Burned-out ruins of railcars after the 1915 hurricane struck Galveston. *Courtesy of the Galveston County Museum.*

Onlookers watching the still smoldering ruins of buildings at the corner of Twenty-Third and Strand Streets after the 1915 hurricane. *Courtesy of the Galveston County Museum.*

The Armour Meatpacking Plant ruins. *Author's collection.*

On Tuesday morning, shortly before 6:00 a.m., a fire was discovered at 2304 Strand Street in a building occupied by the Fred C. Pabst Real Estate Company. The original building where the flames began was that of the Blum Notion Company, which was two stories high; the other buildings consumed in the flames were three stories high.

The flames destroyed all four of the buildings before they were brought under control. They took with them the Blum Notion Company and J.F. Seinsheimer and Company. Sadly, with the destruction of these buildings, Galveston lost the office of the United States Cotton Company and the Knights of Columbus Hall.

The flames from the Blum Notion Company then crossed the alley and consumed the Armour Meat and Swift Packing Plants, totally destroying the buildings, causing $75,000 worth of damage to each. The losses were estimated to cost $50,000 to Blum; $40,000 to Seinsheimer; and $40,000 to Pabst and Reid.

Schadt Hardware Store
September 17, 1917
Mechanic Street, at Twenty-Eighth Street

On Friday, September 17, 1917, just before noon, a watchman discovered a fire near the southwest corner of the hardware store owned by William Schadt.

A short time later, a general alarm was sounded, and all available pieces of firefighting equipment arrived to fight the blaze. By 1:00 p.m., the fire department was successful in controlling the blaze and keeping the fire confined to Mr. Schadt's store. Unfortunately, both the store and the warehouse were both completely destroyed.

The buildings and merchandise were valued at approximately $50,000.

Yurcovich Building/Lyon's Hardware Store
August 30, 1931
2210 Postoffice Street

On Monday, August 30, a fire began in Lyon's Hardware when a gasoline stove exploded. By the time the fire department reached the scene, the three-story building that housed the hardware store was engulfed in flames, as was Nathan's Clothing Store and the Four Seasons Hotel, which occupied the upper floors of the building. Mr. Robert A. Lyon Jr. and his brother W.G. Lyon were both in the store at the time of the explosion; however, Robert Lyon was the only one injured and left in a semiconscious condition. Nearby, in Salzmann's Jewelry Store, the explosion caused display cases to be overturned and cases in J.K. Deat's and Bros. Paint Store to be hurled to the center of the building. In Lyon's Hardware Store, the front plate-glass windows were shattered in the explosion and thrown about.

The proprietors of the nearby Four Seasons Hotel, Mr. and Mrs. Marco Yurcovich, were sent scurrying from the flames. Although the hotel did have one guest checked in, he was not there at the time of the blast. Mr. and Mrs. Yurcovich, the only occupants of the hotel at the time of the blaze, escaped the fire by moving quickly down the front steps. As the blaze began, Mr. Yurcovich was on a second-story back porch, and Mrs. Yurcovich was in a bedroom on the same floor, reading. The blast rocked the building and caused the skylights to explode, sending glass crashing down and flames to shoot in from the first floor. Mrs. Yurcovich rushed to her husband, who had been seriously ill and had difficulty walking. Mrs. Yurcovich managed to get her husband in the screen door and down the front stairs to safety as the flames consumed the building from the back.

Due to the sheer size of the blaze, firefighters carried hoses to the top of the nearby E.S. Levy Building to try to throw a stream on the blaze. It was at this time that a piece of the wall fell on the nearby jewelry storeroom, causing severe damage and one fireman to pass out due to heat exhaustion from the intense flames.

As the fire continued to roar through the hardware store, shotgun shells began to explode and walls began to collapse in the building. The fire then reached through the roof, higher and higher above the building, like a hand reaching toward the sky. Shortly after the fire began, the fire alarm in the E.S. Levy Building began to ring and continued for nearly an hour before the automatic sprinklers started and doused the flames and the entire stock of the store, causing nearly $25,000 worth of damage.

In the aftermath of the blaze, Lyon's Hardware Store, Nathan's Clothing Store, Salzmann's Jewelry Store, E.S. Levy and Company, Eiband's and Star Drugstore had all sustained damage due to the explosion.

As of September 3, the J.W. Zempter Construction Company was busy tearing down the walls of the burned-out building, and plans were being made for a new building to replace it. The original building, owned by Mr. Marco Yurcovich, was built around the turn of the century by Nicholas Clayton and also housed the famed architect's office.

As of September 21, 1932, several insurance companies representing each of the businesses damaged in the explosion sought to sue the gas company for $125,000 for faulty pipes that carried gas to the building. The suit alleged that complaints had been reported several times to the gas company regarding gas leaks, and nothing had been done about it. Since the repairs had never been made, gas escaped and caused the explosion and damage to the Yurcovich Building and surrounding businesses.

E.S. Levy Company Annex
December 26, 1965
516 Twenty-Third Street

On Sunday, December 26, 1965, a fire broke out in the third floor of the Wilder Building, also known as the Levy Annex Building, which housed the offices and children's department of the E.S. Levy Company. The fire

Fighting the flames at the E.S. Levy Annex Building. *Courtesy of Special Collections, Rosenberg Library, Galveston, Texas.*

caused damage to seven businesses, twenty-five apartments and the offices of the E.S. Levy Company, though the main store was not damaged.

The fire began in the ceiling in the northeast corner of the third floor of the building, completely burning it out. The second floor, which housed the company offices, was partially damaged by fire. But most of the damage came from the smoke and water used to extinguish the blaze. The firemen fought the blaze for a little more than four hours before they were finally able to extinguish the flames.

Although twenty-five apartments were damaged, all the residents were able to escape the blaze without injury. The only injuries in the blaze were sustained by one fireman, who had a sliver of glass in his hand. Early estimates of the damage to the building alone determined that it would cost about $75,000 to $100,000. Harry Levy III, speaking as an official of the store, stated that the cost of the damages to equipment was hard to immediately estimate. Levy was quoted as saying, "The building was not gutted, jut ruined. The 1900 storm did not close us; 1915 did not close us, Carla did not close us, and we'll be open as usual." Due to the damage the building sustained, several of Levy's departments were moved across the street and combined.

ABC Racket Store
January 13, 1966
2027 Postoffice Street

Shortly before 10:00 p.m., on Thursday, January 13, 1966, a fire was discovered coming from the back of the ABC Racket Store. Due to the strong winds that were hitting the city, the fire was whipped into a frenzy and began engulfing several buildings in the vicinity. The fire spread from the ABC Racket Store to the nearby Nussenblatt Optometrist at 510 Twenty-First Street, and then it moved on to the Christian Science Reading Room at 512 Twenty-First Street.

The fire destroyed the interiors of both the optometrist's office and the reading room. At the origin of the fire, the Racket Store, three of the four walls of the building remained standing, with all the remaining stock of the

ABC Racket Store/Old Masonic Lodge, circa the 1940s. *Author's collection.*

store damaged by smoke and water. The roofs of all of the buildings were completely burned out.

Upon further investigation, it looked as though the Racket Store had been robbed earlier, and the fire had been set to cover it up. Each of the gun cases and parts of the store containing radios had been ransacked, and a large amount of stock was missing from these areas. The robbers were able to enter the building by cutting through a trapdoor on the roof, and a door at the back of the building, close to where the fire began.

Firemen continued to fight the blaze in a drizzling rain until about 2:00 a.m., when the fire was brought under control. During the blaze, firefighter Howard Pickard suffered from smoke inhalation and firefighter William Klein injured his leg when a ladder slipped.

With destruction of the store also came the destruction of another one of Clayton's architectural treasures, the 1882 Masonic hall, which stood above the store.

The Brass Rail/Stevedore Company Warehouse
January 30, 1978
2410 Strand Street/2213 Water Street

On January 29, 1978, just before 5:00 a.m., a fire was discovered in the McFadden Building in the Brass Rail Restaurant, which occupied the building's second floor. When firefighters and police arrived on the scene, the back door was found to be open, with pry marks evident on the door and frame of the building.

The fire caused a large amount of smoke to rise into the air able to be seen as far as the 5300 block of Broadway Street. The fire department spent several hours pumping nearly 200,000 gallons of water onto the building before the flames were finally arrested. Late that afternoon, the fire department was finally able to leave the scene. Fire officials strongly considered arson the cause of the blaze.

Fifteen hours earlier, on January 29 at about 12:50 p.m., the fire department arrived at the Suderman Stevedore Company Warehouse at 2213 Water Street to find it engulfed in flames. In 1964, the Suderman Stevedore Company took ownership of the one-hundred-year-old building, which was three stories of wooden floors. Unfortunately, due to the intense heat and flames, the structure was weakened and eventually collapsed. It took the fire department 300,000 gallons of water and several hours to get the fire under control.

The combined damage to these buildings was estimated to cost $250,000.

Earlier that month, on January 11, an electrical fire caused about $5,000 worth of damage at the Strand Smoked Meat Company, located at 2122 Strand Street. Due to the increased number of fires in the area, the city planned to implement additional city inspections for construction and plumbing and electrical installation in order to avoid additional fires on Strand Street. Additionally, an officer was regularly assigned to Strand Street to keep the buildings clear of transients.

RESIDENTIAL DISTRICT

Great Fire of Galveston
November 12-13, 1885

On the evening of Thursday, November 12, 1885, a cold northeastern gale blew across Galveston Island, causing the residents to retreat to the warm interiors of their homes. Meanwhile, midway down the block on Strand Street, between Sixteenth and Seventeenth Streets, workers at the Vulcan Iron Foundry began preparing the foundry to close for the evening. The men worked tirelessly, preparing the foundry and bedding down the flames before leaving for the evening. The foundry's workers each left the building and locked it for the night, hurrying to the warmth of their homes and families.

At about 1:30 a.m. on Friday, November 13, 1885, flames were found coming from the rear of the foundry, toward the alley. Between 2:00 and 4:00 a.m., the winds registered a velocity of nearly thirty miles per hour, which caused the flames to be whipped up and blown toward other buildings. Just to the east of the foundry was a large wooden structure, a dwelling that included a store. Flames from the foundry licked the wooden structure until the building was completely enveloped in flames, causing the occupants to race for their lives into the cold night.

Due to the strong winds that were blowing that evening, the flames became a raging fury and reached their fiery tentacles out to anything within reach. Within a few short minutes, a wall of flames was being blown southward across Strand Street, setting a group of wooden buildings on fire. Due to the sounding of a general alarm, the newly formed paid fire

The Galveston fire of '85. *Courtesy of the Library of Congress, microfilm M 3500 M2.3.U6A44.*

department was slow in getting to the fire. Although the fire department fought hard to put the flames out, the strong winds, late alarm and very low water pressure from the new hydrant system hampered its ability to get the fire under control.

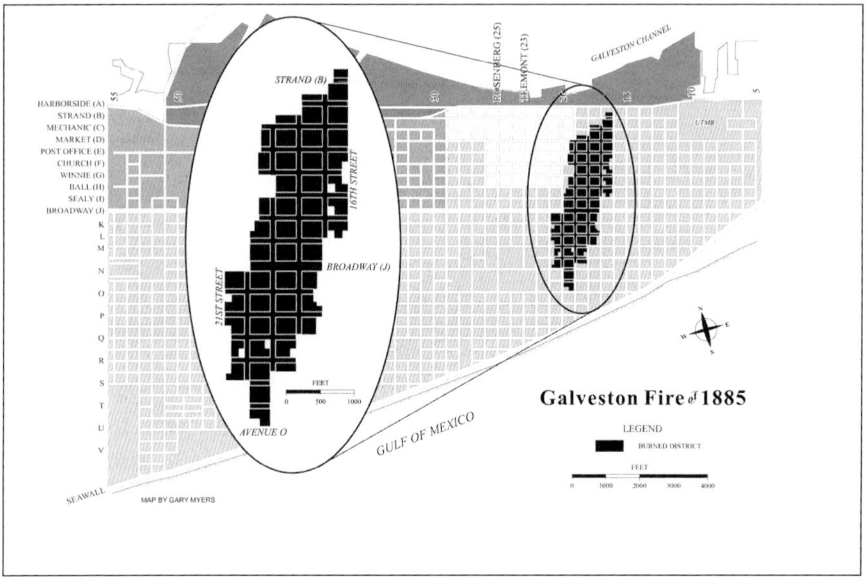

Map of the Great Fire of Galveston, which destroyed forty-two blocks of the city. *Courtesy of Gary Meyers.*

Within moments, the flames, whipped up by the winds, spit embers into the air and onto the roofs of the homes in the area. As the flames increased in intensity and more and more of the residential area was engulfed, residents hurried from their homes, carrying as many of their belongings with them as they could. Residents began to pour buckets of water onto their homes and wet down their roofs almost to no avail. The flames continued to inch farther and farther across Galveston's East End, destroying a variety of dwellings in their path.

The densely populated residential area of Galveston served as fuel for the hungry beast, which continued to inch toward the Gulf of Mexico. The fire continued to consume anything in its way, taking little heed as to what type of structure lay before it. Whether it was a small shack or a large mansion, each was fair game to the appetite of the beast.

The flames would eventually make their way from Strand Street, crossing over to Mechanic Street and continuing up the avenues until they reached Broadway Street. Along the way, the flames licked at the newly constructed post office; however, it was surprisingly spared from the flames. The home of Mr. and Mrs. J.G. Duffield, built in 1885 at 1703 Postoffice Street, was consumed by the flames. As the flames reached Church Street, Mr. and

Top: Looking west over the fire's destruction from Henry Martyn Truehart's home. *Courtesy of Special Collections, Rosenberg Library, Galveston, Texas.*

Bottom: Looking from Leon Blum's home at the devastation caused by the fire. *Courtesy of Special Collections, Rosenberg Library, Galveston, Texas.*

Mrs. Peete watched as their beautiful home at 1618 Church Street was reduced to rubble.

The fire moved like a ravenous beast, engulfing all that it touched. As it approached the brick jail with its slate roof, the prisoners were readied for an evacuation should the need arise. Although the flames licked at the building, it stood firm and survived.

The corner of Strand and Sixteenth Streets. The fire began on the right-hand corner of the image. *Courtesy of Special Collections, Rosenberg Library, Galveston, Texas.*

Inch by inch, the fire's appetite steadily grew, and the wind continued to whip it about. The Walshe family watched in disbelief as their home at 1801 Sealy Street was reduced to ashes within moments; similarly, two blocks up, at 2016 Sealy Street, Mr. and Mrs. Robert F. George watched their beloved home be consumed by the blaze.

The flames, intent on destroying the bustling city, leapt over Broadway Street and consumed the home of Mr. and Mrs. John Z. Scott at 1878 Broadway Street before it continued toward the gulf. By this time, the voracious fire had consumed an area about four blocks wide and nine blocks long, and it did not seem to be slowing. Residents, unable to stop the flames, helped their neighbors by removing whatever items they could carry from their burning homes. Others tried desperately to wet the buildings down with buckets of water in the hopes of saving their homes from the destruction.

At Nineteenth and Postoffice Streets, an elderly gentleman known only as "Old John," who suffering from consumption, was lying in a bed in his home as the flames ravaged toward it. Before neighbors were able to rescue him from the fire, he was found to already be deceased. Surprisingly, his body was not burned; it was believed that he more than likely died from smoke inhalation or shock.

After crossing Broadway Street, the flames continued to consume everything in their path. By the time they reached Avenue O, fuel for the fire was becoming less and less prevalent, causing the flames to reduce in intensity. The fire shrunk from nearly four blocks wide at its widest point to just one block wide by the time it reached Avenue N. Upon reaching Avenue N, the flames began to dwindle until they were finally under control. By 7:00 a.m. on Friday, November 13, the fire had finally been brought under control, and by 9:30 a.m., the flames were completely out.

At one point, nearly two hundred structures were on fire, and nearly twenty-five thousand people were in the streets, trying to assist themselves and their neighbors by removing belongs from the burning dwellings to save them from the flames. In a six-hour period, the flames had consumed an area one mile and one-quarter long, stretching in a southeasterly direction diagonally across the heart of the city.

In the blaze, the business district was thankfully spared; however, 568 structures were consumed across the widespread residential areas of Galveston. The early homes on the island, such as that of Captain James Perry, and several other structures, simple and grand, were lost to the ravages of the fire.

Remnants of houses, chimneys and cisterns in the burned district consumed by the Great Fire. Photographed by P.H. Rose, taken from the November 19, 1885 issue of *Leslie's Weekly*. *Author's collection.*

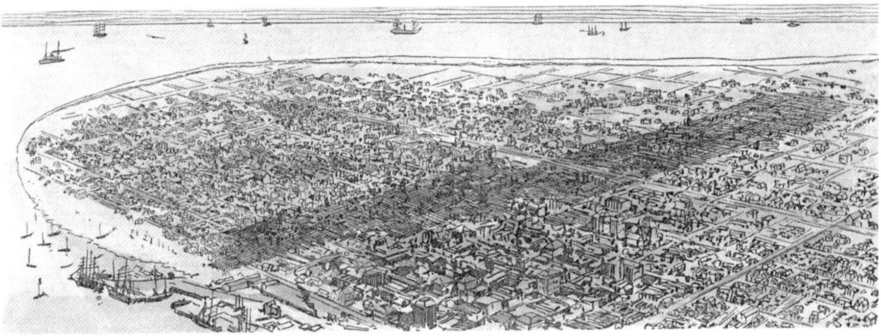

Top: Beach Hotel looking northwest, toward the area consumed by the 1885 fire. Personal collection of Nicholas Clayton, circa 1885. *Courtesy of the Galveston County Museum.*

Bottom: *Harper's Weekly*, November 28, 1885. *The Burnt District, author's collection.*

The next day, as news of the devastation reached other cities, relief committees were already being formed, and nearly $35,000 had already been raised for the relief of those affected by the fire. Throughout the following days and weeks, telegrams of condolences and outpourings of love, along with donations, were received by the city that had been greatly affected by the devastation. Jay Gould pledged $5,000 for the relief of Galveston.

By November 19, the debris had already been cleared, and work had begun to replace the structures that had been lost in the blaze. Shortly after the fire, hundreds of carpenters descended on the island to assist in the recovery and reconstruction of the devastated residential area. Meanwhile, relief committees had been established to systematically render the correct amount of aid to those greatly affected by the blaze.

Within weeks, new structures began to replace those that had burned. Terrified at the thought of another fire destroying her beautiful home,

Rosa Peete had a brick home built with a slate mansard roof to replace the structure she had lost in the great fire.

After the fire, Thomas Goggan and Brothers would publish *The Galveston Fire of '85*, written by Louis Gruetzmacher and Jacob Day, to commemorate the tragedy that befell their great city.

December 21, 1886
Avenue K, Between Twenty-First and Twenty-Second Streets

On Tuesday, December 21, 1886, a fire began in the kitchen of a wood-frame boardinghouse owned by Judge J.H. Barnett and occupied by Mrs. G. Goodwin. The fire started in the early morning hours, between 3:00 a.m. and sunrise.

Reports state that a kerosene lamp was left lit in the kitchen area of the home and fell over, causing an explosion. With great rapidity, the flames progressed and consumed the rear of the boardinghouse and an adjoining two-story structure. Also in flames was the property of Judge Barnett, which was used as a boardinghouse and occupied by R.W. Walston. The servants living in the rear of both of these dwellings were the first to sound the alarm. Unfortunately, a considerable delay occurred in getting the alarm out, even though several shots were fired to attract attention.

At about 3:30 a.m., a general alarm was received by the fire department from box 71, and the department hurried to the scene. Before the fire department arrived, a third structure on the property caught fire, causing a huge flaming spectacle. Due to a light southwesterly wind, the flames from the three buildings were spread northeast. Several structures on the block north of where the fire originated already had embers landing on their roofs and were set ablaze, causing their occupants to hurry to the streets to watch as their effects burned in the blaze.

Finally, the homes of Isidor Holstein, Professor Lindenborg and Mr. F. Egert became consumed in the blaze. With the fire billowing as quickly as it did, it was not long before the homes of H. Wurtzburger, A.H. Rosenfeld, Mrs. A. Jacobs and George F. Schneider Jr. were also brought into the blaze. Due to the fact that the Schneider home was on the corner of Avenue K and Twenty-First Street, the blaze was checked by the street. The buildings on the east side of Twenty-First Street, though saved from the flames, were badly scorched.

The fire department worked hard to contain the flames; however, it was hampered by the delay in the alarm and the time it took to look for a cistern or source of water to contain the flames. Due to the intense heat, the heated atmosphere caused the wind to pick up and carry sparks as far as Strand Street and the harbor. By this time, numerous citizens had arrived on the scene and began removing personal effects from the homes to help those in need. The residents on the south side of the block, between Broadway Street and Avenue K, were able to save very little of their household goods; however, those on the north side, facing Broadway Street, were able to move items from their homes and place them in the esplanades; however, due to the heat and flying embers, the fire continued to move along the south side of Broadway Street, consuming more homes.

While the fire continued to progress down the block, several structures did actually survive the flames, including the Baptist church on the southeast corner of Broadway and Twenty-Second Streets and the homes of Mrs. Levy and several of her neighbors. These were the only structures saved on the north side of the block. On the south side of the block, only one of the seven lots still contained structures. These were the cottages of Mr. Masor and Mr. L. Lockhart. The cottage of Mr. Lockhart was badly scorched and partially burned. Out of the sixteen structures on the block, only five were saved.

On the block bounded by Avenues J and K and Twenty-First and Twenty-Second Streets, the fire consumed nineteen structures and left only six partially damaged. On Broadway Street, two stores were threatened by sparks to their roofs; however, quick action by the fire department saved the buildings from being consumed in the blaze. By about 6:00 a.m., the flames were nearly out, as the fire had reached Broadway Street and Avenue L and had run out of fuel.

Considering the loss of structures and household belongings, the damage was estimated to cost $80,000.

January 20, 1963
2320 Avenue G

Shortly before 6:00 a.m. on Sunday, January 20, 1963, a fire of unknown origins began in a three-story wood-frame apartment home with thirteen occupants. A passing motorist saw the building on fire and flagged down Patrolman James Beatty to alert him. The patrolman rushed to the scene to lend a hand; however, he was unable to get close to the home due to the flames and heat emanating from the burning building. Within moments,

Beatty saw tenants evacuating the building. Many of them jumped from the upper floors of the building.

When the fire department arrived on the scene, Joe Abraham and Fire Captain Arthur Holland were able to rescue one of the tenants by driving their truck next to the burning building to serve as a shield as they pulled the man to safety.

One of the survivors stated that he smelled smoke about three hours earlier and that he and another tenant searched their floors but found no signs of fire or where the smoke was coming from, so they both returned to bed. Around about 5:45 a.m., T.O. Mathis was awakened by another tenant, Lyle Fleming, and he saw smoke coming in from beneath his door. Mathis rushed to call the fire department; however, just as he reached the phone, the entire hall burst into flames. He had to hurry to evacuate the building. Along the way, he notified two other residents and helped them to safely escape the burning building.

The fire department was able to quickly put the fire out, and thankfully, due to the fact that the home had an empty lot on either side, no other structures were damaged in the blaze. Upon further inspection, it was found that the fire was most likely started by a heater, as the night was so cold. All signs pointed to it starting on the west side of the structure on the ground floor and being fanned toward the upper floors. As the residents began to evacuate the building, the open door allowed more air to flow into the building, which allowed the flames to increase in intensity.

After the fire, all that was left of the structure were a couple of walls that were later torn down with a winch truck. A search of the debris was done in order to locate anyone else who may have been a victim to the fire. Upon searching the rubble, four victims were found: two women and two men. The rest of the residents received treatment at John Sealy Hospital.

December 12, 1967
1908 Church Street

On Tuesday, December 12, 1967, at about 4:46 p.m., a fire began to consume a nineteen-room apartment home on Church Street. The fire department arrived on the scene and began to fight the blaze, but it had difficulty, as the flames were between the walls and ceilings of the building. Thankfully, all thirteen residents of the structure were able to escape, uninjured. However, the apartment home received about $25,000 worth of damage.

It was believed that the fire started on the first floor in a northeast room, where a space heater had become separated from its flexible hose. The fire then traveled to a storage closet in the room, where it burned through the ceiling and then began to travel between the walls to the upper floors. The roof of the home began collapsing, starting in the alleyway and working its way forward.

Two nearby structures were threatened by the fire: the Debanlis Apartments and the building that housed Murillo Photo Studios. Firemen worked tirelessly with nearly every piece of equipment to save the nearby structures and to extinguish the blaze. They fought the blaze until about 8:30 p.m., when it was finally brought under control. Many firemen remained on scene to guard what few possessions of the residents remained after the fire. Thankfully, only two people were injured in the blaze: one a bystander, who was assisting the firemen when glass broke from an upper floor and fell, cutting his hand; and a fireman who was hit with a hose in the right eye, cutting his skin.

January 7, 1971
1319 Thirty-First Street

On Thursday, January 7, 1971, at 12:19 a.m., a fire was reported in a two-story home with an attic. The house contained five apartments: two in the basement, two on the ground floor and one in the attic. At the time of the fire, it was believed that all the residents of the home had escaped. Firemen arrived on the scene at about 12:30 a.m. and battled the blaze heroically.

At about 6:40 a.m., the firefighters were finally able to enter the attic apartment, which was filled with a very thick, acrid smoke. Upon entering the attic, the firefighters discovered the body of Mr. James Richardson on the floor. It was believed that he had died from smoke inhalation and carbon monoxide poisoning. Being unable to leave the fire, Mr. Richardson received severe burns over his entire body.

It was believed that the cause of the blaze was a heater that had been knocked over and pulled away from the open gas jet. The investigation showed that the fire probably started on the stairs leading to the attic apartment. The roof of the building was completely burned off, and the damage to the attic and the main floor of the house was estimated to cost $10,500.

May 2, 1975
Twenty-Seventh and Postoffice Streets

On Friday, May 2, 1975, at about 11:22 p.m., two officers, T.L. Kirkpatrick and Joseph Faust, discovered a fire in a boardinghouse at 509 Twenty-Seventh Street. They entered the home and began to alert the boarders of the fire, but they were thwarted from entering the second floor due to the heat and smoke. To their knowledge, everyone had evacuated the building, including a man who jumped from a second-story window and another who attempted to climb down a tree near the dwelling.

Upon their arrival at the scene, nine trucks and several firefighters began to secure the area by notifying nearby residents of the fire, securing their buildings and getting them a safe distance from the fire. They also rescued another occupant from the second floor.

After the fire, it was determined that four buildings, 511 Twenty-Seventh Street, 2701 Avenue E, 2703 Avenue E and 509 Twenty-Seventh Street, were consumed in the blaze. Sadly, after the fire had been extinguished the next morning, a woman's body was discovered at 509 Twenty-Seventh Street.

WHARF DISTRICT

October 11, 1892
Creosote Factory/Pier 29

At 4:30 a.m. on Tuesday, October 11, 1892, a fire started at Pier 29 from the creosote factory. The fire erupted on the north side of the building, near a pile of lumber. An eyewitness reported that the fire burst like a powder magazine exploding. As the flames erupted, they shot out rapidly in all directions.

Considerable damage was done to the creosote factory and its contents, but thankfully, none of the nearby ships or stored cotton was damaged. As the light of day approached, the true destruction of the fire was revealed. Timbers and barrels showed signs of charring on their exteriors, but luckily, the barrels were not destroyed. The large creosoting cylinder that had fallen over was badly warped and reddened by the fire. The large supporting braces that held the tank were badly warped, causing the tank to lean precariously, threatening to fall over.

Harbor and Bay Streets, looking west (*top*) and east (*bottom*), circa 1907. *Author's collection.*

At the outbreak of the fire, thirteen steamers were docked at the surrounding piers. Combined, these ships held nearly thirty thousand bales of cotton that miraculously survived the fire. While there was wind blowing, the wind did not blow embers toward the cotton bales.

The firemen dutifully fought the flames and sprayed streams of water on the bales of cotton nearby. Had it not been for their work, the fire could have consumed the ships, cotton, buildings and wharf, which would have cost nearly $5 million.

Mallory Steamship Company Warehouses
July 2, 1896
2400 Block of Avenue A

On Thursday, July 2, 1896, at about 1:10 p.m., the citizens of Galveston watched in horror as a fire erupted on the wharf. In less than an hour, it reduced four blocks of the wharf front to ashes. Today, this area would be situated at the 2400 block of Avenue A, or Harborside Drive, as it is currently known.

The fire originated at the foot of Twenty-Fifth Street and spread in both directions rapidly, destroying everything in its path, as the wharf sheds were dry. The sheds of the Mallory Wharf Line, sitting at the water's edge, were built in 1887 by Henry Devlin for the New York and Texas Steamship Company. They were both destroyed. The largest of the sheds was 1,200 feet long and 100 feet wide. The other shed was about one-third the size of the other.

These warehouses contained a little over 2,300 sacks of wool and 125 bales of compressed cotton, as well as 2,000 rolls of bagging and some general merchandise. The warehouse was full during this fire because earlier in the week, the steamship *Conche* had emptied its cargo at the Mallory Docks for shipment at a later date.

The Galveston Wharf Company lost extensive property along the waterfront, including warehouses and sheds extending from Twenty-Fifth to

Mallory Wharf fire. *Author's collection.*

Twenty-Eighth Streets. The damage to the wharves was extensive, and they needed to be completely rebuilt.

Additional damage from the fire caused a loss of twenty-six freight cars that belonged to the Gulf, Colorado and Santa Fe Railroad and the International and Great Northern Railroad. Five thousand bales of jute and a large amount of bagging and ties were also lost.

While there were a number of theories as to what could have caused the fire, in the end, it was determined that the cause of the fire was caused by the spontaneous combustion of wool. The damage to the property and the loss of the merchandise in the warehouses was estimated to cost between $200,000 and $300,000.

The Mallory Steamship Company; the Gulf, Colorado and Santa Fe Railway; and the Galveston Wharf Company planned to rebuild what was lost, replace everything and open in time for the cotton season that fall.

Galveston Wharf
January 23, 1909
Piers 12 and 13

At about 8:08 p.m. on Friday, January 22, 1909, a fire alarm was sounded from box 166 at Pier 12. It was said that the watchman had just pulled the box from Pier 12 and was in a small office on the south end of the pier when the watchman's lamp exploded in the office of the Union Telegraph Company of Pier 12, causing a major conflagration on Piers 12 and 13.

Within ten minutes of the explosion, the fire had made considerable headway and was threatening nearby wharfs and docked ships. To avoid the threat of the flames, the captains of the *Shira* and the *Indian* deftly moved their vessels from the pier and out into the channel.

The Galveston Wharf Company, the owner of Pier 12, built it as a double pier, meaning it contained both Piers 12 and 13, and it was operated by Langbehn Bros. Due to a slight southeast wind, the flames were coming under control; however, the intensity of the flames threatened to burn Pier 10 as well as Elevator A.

Pier 12, an immense building, was open at both ends due to its height and length. The wind whipped through the building, causing the fire to grow in intensity and heat. While over twenty streams of water were thrown on the fire, immense clouds of smoke billowed across the water and covered Pier 14 and Elevator A, which were located immediately west of the fire. The fire continued to engulf the building and the pilings that held it. Within a very brief period, the entire pier was consumed, save for a small corner of the building.

A clerk who worked at Pier 12 made a daring rescue of papers and pet monkeys, which made their home in the pier's office. The clerk jumped through a window, grabbed the monkeys and particularly important paperwork and then broke back through the window before the flames consumed the office.

Pier 10, located just to the east of the conflagration, was in danger of being completely destroyed due to the intense heat coming from the sheds and oil burning on the pier. Thankfully, a stream of water was sprayed on the burning shed, which allowed the flames to be brought under control. Meanwhile, barges of lumber were still in the slip east of the burning pier. Men worked feverishly, pulling water from the harbor and dumping it on the lumber to keep it from burning. Had the barges been caught, the fire would have raged out of control, and Pier 10 would have been lost as well.

Within moments of the alarm, the fire department raced to the fire, doing its best to keep the flames from reaching other buildings, as they did not have a fire boat to fight the fire from the water. Thankfully, already in the water was the *Ima Hogg*, a steamer that belonged to Suderman and Dolson, which had its own firefighting equipment. Due to its location on the water, the ship was able to spray streams of water on the northern side of the pier and Elevator A. With the assistance of the *Ima Hogg*, the fires were able to be fought from multiple sides, bringing the threat of fire under control. This allowed the fire department to focus on other areas of the fire.

As the fire continued to engulf the sheds of the piers, the engines of the Port of Galveston Railroad made rapid work of racing into the burning buildings, hooking onto the cars and pulling them from the fire.

The fire, which had started at 8:00 p.m., was still raging around midnight. Nearly every piece of firefighting equipment was working to control the fire, and the *Ima Hogg* continued to fight the fire from the water below. Due to the valiant efforts of the fire department and the crew of the *Ima Hogg*, the fire was finally brought under control, and the flames were extinguished.

It was estimated that Piers 12 and 13 were totally destroyed and that the bulkheads of the pier were damaged. The damage would cost at least \$60,000 to repair. Yet the damage to building, the freight and the nearby structures was estimated to cost \$425,000.

Galveston Wharf Company
May 30, 1920
Pier 41

Late in the afternoon of Monday, May 30, a large fire broke out at a large warehouse, causing considerable damage to the Port of Galveston. The warehouse, located at Pier 41, contained a large cargo of sisal that was stored in the north end of pier.

The large concrete warehouse, owned by the Galveston Wharf Company, was leased by the Cotton Concentration Company. The fire was estimated to have caused nearly $1.5 million worth of damage to the warehouse and its contents and nearly $3 million worth of damage to the sisal that was stored in the warehouse.

The fire originally broke out on the south end of the warehouse, on the upper floor in section C. The flames completely consumed the sisal stored within the warehouse. While no definite cause could be given for the fire, it was believed that the sisal spontaneously combusted from its exposure to the heat in the warehouse. Tremendous flames raging on the floor above caused the sisal on the floor below to also catch fire. After several hours of being exposed to the intense heat and flames, the second floor of the warehouse collapsed on the lower floor.

Double-decker Pier 41, circa 1918. *Author's collection.*

Pier 41 was destroyed by fire. The fire started on the second floor in sisal storage. The building was constructed in 1915–16. *Courtesy of Special Collections, Rosenberg Library, Galveston, Texas.*

Firefighters feared that the existing oil pipes, which ran beneath the pier from the Mexican Fuel Oil Corporation, might catch fire; therefore, they had a stream of water from the *Charles Clarke* sprayed on the pipes to keep them cool.

By the early morning, the fire was contained; however, it smoldered for several days afterward. Various bits of equipment and the *Charles Clarke* were still in the vicinity, spraying streams of water on the smoldering ruins to combat the fire.

Texas Sulphur Company *September 30, 1920* *Pier 35*

At about 1:40 a.m., Ed McCarty, a fireman on a barge at Pier 38, stated that he saw smoke and flames in the fire bin at the sulfur plant. He believed that the fire at Pier 35, which was made of wood, was the result of an explosion. The flames began to spread rapidly, due in part to the high winds that were blowing at nearly thirty miles an hour. The fire hungrily consumed all that was in its path, including the loading devices the flames originated on. About

Top: Pier 35 Sulphur Yards. *Author's collection.*

Bottom: The remains of Pier 35 after the fire. *Courtesy of Special Collections, Rosenberg Library, Galveston, Texas.*

fifteen railcars full of cotton and forty cars on the tracks at the sulfur plant were also consumed in the blaze. A nearby Italian vessel, the *Etna*, had its cargo of wheat catch fire.

Upon their arrival at the pier, nearly forty firefighters were affected by the fumes of the burning sulfur, and Captain Thibedeaux was struck by a flying

The remains of Sulphur Yards and its equipment after the fire at Pier 35. *Courtesy of Special Collections, Rosenberg Library, Galveston, Texas.*

timber (afterward, he was taken to his home). At about 3:15 a.m., Fire Chief Ryan stated that another explosion occurred inside the plant, and he said it was caused by several oil containers.

Destroyed in the blaze was the Texas Gulf Sulfur company. The Anchor Milling Plant had its cottonseed grinding plant destroyed in the blaze. And the Cotton Concentration Company, which adjoined Pier 35, was partially destroyed.

Other vessels within the vicinity of the fire were quickly moved away in order to save them and their cargos from destruction. Due to the firewall on the east side of the pier, Pier 36 was saved from the fire.

Galveston Wharf Company/Mallory Line Docks
January 14, 1926
Piers 23, 24, 25 and 26

Shortly after 11:00 p.m., a disastrous fire broke out at the Mallory Line Wharves between Piers 23, 24, 25 and 26. The fire began on the north end of the building with a bale of smoldering cotton. Within about ten minutes of the blaze being discovered, the flames had burned through the roof and were sending flames and smoke skyward.

The sheds and docks were filled with merchandise that belonged to the Oklahoma Cotton Growers' Association and other shippers. While the warehouses had been well cleaned out earlier, there were still about one thousand bales of cotton that were stored between Twenty-Fifth and Twenty-Sixth Streets. This shipment was scheduled to depart on the *Concho*, which had been moored in port. However, the ship was moved into the channel to protect it from the fire.

Around Twenty-Fifth Street there is a firebreak wall that divides the building, and it held until the wind caused the flames to shift northwest, over the wall, to the cotton bales stored there. As the flames broke through the roof, several railcars filled with cotton and sulfur also caught fire, creating fumes that hampered the efforts of the firefighters. By 12:35 p.m., the flames began to totally consume the warehouse and all that was stored in the area.

To slow the spread of the flames, strings of cars in and around the sheds were moved away, but this hampered the firefighters from getting to the flames at the Twenty-Fifth Street crossing. Shortly after 1:15 a.m., the flames died down and were finally put in check, though major damage had already been done to the port and Mallory Wharf. The damage to the wharf was

Mallory Wharf after the fire. *Courtesy of Special Collections, Rosenberg Library, Galveston, Texas.*

Galveston Waterfront fire. *Author's collection.*

estimated by George Sealy, vice-president of the Galveston Wharf Company, to cost $50,000. The cotton lost by the Cotton Concentration Company was estimated to cost $500,000. The actual cost of the damage was higher, due to other merchandise that had been stacked in the area lost to the flames.

April 26, 1973
Pier 10

At about 12:40 a.m. on Thursday, April 26, 1973, a fire erupted in the Pier 10 warehouse, which contained about eleven thousand bales of cotton, each of which was valued at about $150. The two adjoining warehouses on the south end of the building were saved due to a firewall that divided them. The flames from the warehouse towered hundreds of feet into the night sky and could be seen from miles away, even out on the west end of the island.

When firemen arrived on the scene, the warehouse was completely engulfed in flames with smoke rising into the air. Forty-seven members of the Galveston Fire Department were sent to John Sealy Hospital for treatment on their eyes due to the cotton lint–filled smoke. The fire was so large that assistance was provided by the coast guard and the Hitchcock and La Marque Volunteer Fire Departments.

Water was pumped in from nearby hydrants and the bay in order to extinguish the massive blaze. By midday, the flames had subsided, and the fire was contained. Firemen and dockworkers began removing the bales, most of which were still smoldering, to vacant lots on Thirty-Third and Forty-First Streets. It was there that they were again soaked with water to keep them from smoldering.

The damage to the building and cotton was estimated to cost $1.5 million.

WAREHOUSE DISTRICT

Gulf Colorado and Santa Fe Railway Roundhouse and Repair Shops
January 30, 1889
Mechanic and Fortieth Streets

At 4:00 a.m. on Wednesday, January 30, 1889, the city of Galveston suffered another devastating blow. The fire started in the roundhouse of the Gulf Colorado and Santa Fe Railroad and machine shops, which were located at the extreme western end of Galveston, near Fortieth Street. An engineer who was working near the Mallory Wharf that night along with several others noticed the flames and rushed to the scene to help in whatever way possible.

A general alarm was sounded, and the fire company responded quickly. Engineer Bark was working in the machine shop, which shared a roof with the roundhouse, when someone cried, "Fire!" He emerged from the machine shop to find the entire building in flames. Due to the rapid consumption of the building by the fire, Bark made a hasty retreat from the structure for his own safety.

When the firefighters arrived, the building was so consumed by flames that they could do little to try to save it. In a search for water, the company determined that the twenty-five-thousand-gallon cistern contained within the burning building and the well were too close to the fire to be used. A smaller cistern was used; however, the supply of water was quickly used up and sent the fire department scrambling in search of more water. An attempt was made to take water from the bay, but since it was low tide, there was not enough suction to pump it. Finally, a bucket brigade was formed, and the men worked to save the smaller buildings nearby.

Unfortunately, the roundhouse, which had become a massive ball of fire, contained ten engines and tenders fully loaded with coal and water that were lost in the flames, as they were unable to be removed from the roundhouse.

By the time the fire was extinguished, the roundhouse and maintenance shop were reduced to ashes. The loss of the engines, buildings, machinery, tools and other items was estimated to cost $75,000—$25,000 of that is attributed to the loss of the two switch engines, five passenger engines and three freight engines that were estimated to cost about $2,500 a piece. Thankfully, all other buildings on the property—the car repair shops, the machine shops and the car sheds, which were filled with passenger coaches—were saved from the flames.

Gulf, Colorado and Santa Fe Railroad Car Shops
May 7, 1891
Mechanic and Thirty-Seventh Streets

Shortly after 3:00 a.m. on Friday, May 7, 1891, a fire was discovered at the machine shops of the Gulf, Colorado and Santa Fe Railroad, located at Thirty-Seventh and Mechanic Streets. The glowing blaze of the fire was seen by the chief of the Galveston Fire Department from across the city, and he ended up sounding the fire alarm. By the time the fire company arrived, the car shed was completely engulfed in flames, along with a number of coaches, which were sitting on a spur alongside the shed.

Two years before, a fire had struck the company's roundhouse and machine shed, destroying the machine sheds. After the destruction of the building, the mechanical department was transferred to the car shops, which had been destroyed in the fire. While the exact cause of the blaze was not known, it was determined that the fire originated in the oil and waste storeroom, located at the northeastern end of the shop. The office for the mechanical department was located at the other end of the shed and was seriously damaged in the blaze, causing the loss of time checks, books and papers.

All of the buildings were constructed of wood, and the fire rapidly consumed them, as well as the cars and engines that were stored under its roof and nearby. A couple of the cars were Pullman cars, and there was an old pay car, two engines that were being repaired and several boxcars loaded with oil. Unfortunately, the flames caused the barrels of oil to explode, which caused the fire to increase in intensity and push the firefighters farther away, unable to get near the fire to put it out. Thankfully, due to the diligence of the firefighters, the paint shop, which had four new coaches under its roof; the storehouse; and the workshop that sat near the machine shop were spared from the destruction of the fire.

By 5:00 a.m., the fire was put out, and it was determined that it destroyed the 68-foot-by-270-foot machine shop, several Pullman cars and freight cars and tools that belonged to employees. Except for the tools, all of the losses belonged to the Gulf, Colorado and Santa Fe Company and were estimated to cost $85,000.

The company had plans to rebuild not only the machine shop but also the building in which it housed its passenger coaches.

Cotter and Steinbrink Planing Mills February 28, 1893

At about 4:20 a.m. on the morning of February 28, 1893, a fire broke out at the Cotter and Steinbrink Planing Mills situated on the west end of Mechanic Street. Due to a stiff breeze blowing from the bay, the flames were whipped up. By the time the fire companies arrived on the scene, the property was completely engulfed in flames. The fire burned all that came within its path. As the fire consumed the property, the flames and sparks reached across the street to eight wood-frame dwellings, causing severe damage to them all.

By the time the fire was extinguished, it was determined that no insurance was by carried by John A. Cotter and Frederick W. Steinbrink, and their loss of several pieces of equipment, structures and the materials stored within them was not covered.

After the fire was completely extinguished, it was determined that the loss of the mill would cost between $12,000 and $15,000, and the loss of the eight wood-frame structures would cost about $8,000.

This was not the first time Cotter and Steinbrink had dealt with the threat of fire. On February 22, 1896, flames broke out on this same spot and destroyed everything in their path. The owners, although they carried no insurance, decided to rebuild and went into debt to the tune of about $700, which was paid off before the year was out.

W.F. Ladd Warehouse October 25, 1896

In a two-story brick warehouse owned by William F. Ladd, bounded by Twenty-Ninth, Thirtieth, Postoffice and Market Streets, there was a devastating fire—the most disastrous cotton fire to hit Galveston at this point. This warehouse sat in the heart of the warehouse district and was surrounded by the Factor's Warehouse Company, the Gulf City Compress and the Taylor Compress Company.

The time at which the fire officially started was never determined, as the watchman did not sound the alarm until well after the fire started. Several fire companies saw the blaze and left well before the alarm was sounded. The official alarm came from box 123 at the corner of Thirtieth and Postoffice Streets and Police Officer Rhodes. Another alarm was sounded by Officer Smith at box 24 on Twenty-Ninth and Mechanic Streets.

Compress ruins at Thirtieth at Market Streets. *Courtesy of Special Collections, Rosenberg Library, Galveston, Texas.*

When the official alarm sounded from the waterworks station, Company No. 8 already had a stream of water on the fire. That evening, the battle to stop the blaze was a hard-fought one, as there was a strong northerly breeze blowing, causing the fire to spread rapidly. Among the first to arrive at the scene was Chief Ernst Wegner and Assistant Chief Gernand, who both sent out a general alarm, calling the fire companies to the fire. Within a short time, numerous water streams were put on the blaze in the hopes of getting the flames under control.

As the fire had grown large, bales of cotton across the street, in front of the Taylor Compress, began to ignite. Several firefighters fought for over an hour to put out the bales, and then they turned their attentions to the blaze. The fire sent an immense shower of sparks high into the sky. These sparks landed on the nearby buildings, where cotton was also stored. It seemed nearly impossible, but the firemen were able to contain the blaze to the warehouse. Several walls of the warehouse began to crash as the fire gained strength.

Across the alley from the fire was a one-story wooden cottage that was crushed by a falling wall. Thankfully, all the occupants of the home owned by Charles Gardner were able to escape injury shortly after being warned of the impending danger.

Chief Wegner sustained an injury when he stepped on a nail that went through his boot and into his foot. After trying to keep his post for a long time, the pain got so unbearable that the chief finally agreed to have his foot examined. Due the seriousness of the injury, he was unable to resume his duties for several days.

In all, the total loss to the buildings and the cotton was estimated to cost $150,000.

Merchants and Planters Compress May 16, 1914

In 1874, a charter was granted to the Gulf City Cotton Press and Manufacturing Company, which located its facility in the three city blocks bounded by Twenty-Ninth, Thirty-Third, Winnie and Sealy Streets. By 1885, these blocks were filled with the buildings and yards of the company.

By 1890, the company had a storage space for cotton in its yards—enough for twenty-six thousand bales of cotton. The Gulf City Cotton Press and Manufacturing Company later became the Merchants and Planters Compress.

West Yard Merchants and Planters Compress, pre-1900. *Author's collection.*

In 1914, a fire began in the west warehouse of the compress, which was storing eleven thousand bales of cotton at the time. By the time the fire was discovered by William Irvin, a watchman, it had already consumed much of the cotton and the building. When the fire alarm was sounded, the fire department rushed to the scene to find the entire block completely engulfed by flames. The fire was so intense that it burned out of control and threatened to destroy the building.

While the origin of the fire was not able to be determined, it was known that it started in the southwest corner of the warehouse. It continued to burn, consuming all the cotton in the warehouse as the fire department used several streams of water to try to control it. As the fire department fought the blaze, several bits of wall fell, causing firemen, including Chief Gernand, to jump out of the way. Unfortunately, a man—possibly a longshoreman—was not so lucky, as a portion of the wall collapsed on him, burying him beneath the rubble and ash. The firemen worked frantically to remove him from the debris and assess his injuries. As he was in critical condition, the man was rushed to John Sealy Hospital, where he was pronounced dead upon arrival.

At about 1:30 a.m., the fire was finally under control. Only the west warehouse was lost to the blaze; the north, south and east warehouses were spared. Per Daniel W. Kempner, the warehouse was nearly half full with eleven thousand to twelve thousand bales of cotton that had accumulated due to the slow movement of shipments. When all was said and done, it was estimated that the damage to the building and cotton cost $900,000.

K. Tidemann and Company Sheds
March 7, 1915

A fire broke out in the concentration sheds of K. Tidemann and Company, located between Thirty-Fourth and Thirty-Fifth Streets and Avenues D and E. Night Watchman Robert Burns was making his rounds when he noticed a fire had started on the exterior of the building, facing Thirty-Fifth Street. He hurried to get a hose to try to extinguish the flames; however, he noticed that the fire was soon going to be out of his control. It was then that he called the Galveston Brewery, which turned the call in to the fire department.

The blaze began at 12:26 a.m., and the entire fire department rushed to the scene. As soon as the fire department arrived, nearly a dozen streams of water were pointed at the fire to get it under control. The fire department was fighting a blaze with strong winds from the north, which fanned the flames higher and higher. Two boxcars near the sheds were destroyed, along with their contents. An earlier fire about a month prior had damaged the cotton picker, which was also owned by K. Tidemann and Company sat to the east of the shed.

Fire Chief Gernand and his crew handled the fire quickly and efficiently and kept the fire from spreading to nearby buildings. All morning, the fire department fought tirelessly to keep the flames in check and to put the fire out. As of midday, although the building was in ruins and mounds of charred cotton lay about, the fire was under control, and there was no pressing threat. In all there were about $300,000 worth of damages between the cotton and the shed. The shed was a total loss and cost about $6,000 to replace. The cotton, about six thousand bales, was also damaged, which comprised the bulk of the loss. Thankfully, it was all covered by insurance.

Moody Cotton Compress
October 11, 1931
Forty-Ninth and Broadway Streets

On the afternoon of Sunday, October 11, 1931, a fire broke out at the twenty-one-acre Moody Cotton Compress at Forty-Ninth and Broadway Streets on the far western side of the complex. The blaze originated in the 1927 warehouse that had been built by M.C. Bowden for the Moody Cotton Compress Complex, and it destroyed nearly thirteen thousand bales of cotton, causing nearly $500,000 worth of damage. At the time, the Moody Cotton Compress was the largest and most modern compress of its kind, serving as a model to others around the country.

Gabe Himler, a watchman at the complex, discovered the fire in the second section of the warehouse. At the time of its discovery, the fire had just started, and Himler tried to put it out with a bucket of water. As the

Firemen spraying the flames of the Moody Compress fire. *Courtesy of the Austin Smith Collection.*

Smoke billowing from the Moody Compress Cotton fire. *Courtesy of Special Collections, Rosenberg Library, Galveston, Texas.*

flames grew, Himler called a second watchman, Dave Dugan, and they both tried to douse the flames with a fire hose, but to no avail. As the fire grew, so did the column of smoke rising above the building, which attracted the attention of Fire Company No. 6 at Thirty-Seventh and Broadway Streets, which hurried to the scene of the blaze.

Within ten minutes of the alarm being sounded, the blaze had already spread to two sections of the building and was gaining speed. Although the fire began in the second section of the building, the flames spread to the first and third sections, devouring everything in its path. Due to the firewall in the third section of the building, the fire was kept from moving into the other sections of the building. In the first section of the building, closest to Broadway Street, the fire was kept in check until the wall finally collapsed and allowed the flames to enter the open area outside. Due to a brisk wind blowing, the flames were whipped up and thrust higher and higher into the night sky.

The fire burned throughout the night and into the morning in three of the 1,100-square-foot warehouse's seven sections. The men fought the blaze bravely, and by Monday evening, they were able to withdraw from the fire as the salvage crews arrived on the scene to try to save as much cotton as was possible.

The concrete building had suffered much damage, and the roof caved in. Damage to the building, which was originally valued at $330,000, was estimated to cost $100,000.

As the firemen fought the blaze, six men were injured, four of whom were firemen. Of the firemen hurt, Tony Napoli was considered to have the most serious injury: a crushed foot. The other firemen dealt with minor burns and smoke in their eyes. Fire Marshal V.E. Frederickson Jr. was supplying gas to several pumpers fighting the blaze when his car and a gasoline container inside it ignited. Fireman E. Topping was injured when a ladder fell and struck him. While no one was seriously injured, they were all treated for their injuries at John Sealy Hospital.

Cotton Concentration Company May 25, 1943

At 10:45 p.m. on the night of May 24, 1943, during a rainstorm, a thunderbolt struck the door of a warehouse that belonged to the Cotton Concentration Company at Fifty-Ninth Street. Rosa Lee Lofton, the wife of an employee of the company who lived near the building, saw the lightning bolt strike the heavy metal door of the building and bounce to a spot fifty feet away. Lofton also stated that after the lightning struck, she, too, was knocked down by the force of the blast.

After the blast struck the building in section E, a general alarm was sent out, calling all the fire companies to the scene to fight the fire. A number of coast guardsmen also arrived to assist in fighting the flames. In all, it took nearly 350 city firemen, 200 U.S. Coast Guardsmen and several auxiliary firemen to bring the flames under control and put them out.

The fire consumed nearly seven thousand bales of cotton, causing damage that was unofficially estimated to cost between $75,000 and $100,000. The fire, which raged through the night, continued to burn and caused several firemen to receive treatment at John Sealy Hospital for severely reddened eyes. The fire continued burning for nearly six hours before it was brought under control.

The body of night watchman George Homer Hardeman, sixty-eight, was found at the scene by a fireman around 6:45 a.m., nearly eight hours after the fire started. It seems that Hardeman had put the key in the ADT

Cotton sheds of the Cotton Concentration Company. *Courtesy of Special Collections, Rosenberg Library, Galveston, Texas.*

box; however, his death was a bit of a mystery. Although multiple doors to the building were open, Hardeman was found forty feet inside the building, near the fire door.

Bluebonnet Warehouse
April 20, 1975
3802 Water Street

On Sunday, after being notified of a fire at 4:51 p.m., ninety-six firefighters, including firefighters from La Marque and Galveston's west end, were on the scene to fight the tremendous blaze, which consumed the Bluebonnet Warehouse on Water Street. The warehouse, which was storing between six thousand and seven thousand bales of cotton, was ignited when a low motor backfired. Every bale of cotton was destroyed in the blaze, while only half of the warehouse was damaged, thanks to a fire wall that stopped the flames.

Firemen fighting the blaze at the Bluebonnet Warehouse fire. *Author's collection.*

However, due to a northerly wind, the embers were lifted into the air and ignited one hundred bales in the other half of the building.

By 1:00 a.m., the blaze was brought under control, and thirty firefighters were taken to John Sealy Hospital for smoke inhalation and eye injuries, none of which were serious. After the fire, crews were busy wetting down the bales to ensure that the fire was completely stopped and that no hotspots or bales were still smoldering. After the blaze, Piers 37 and 38 were shut down due to the fact that the fire hydrants to those piers were without water.

Farmers Export Grain Company
December 27, 1977

At about 8:30 p.m., an explosion rocked the Port of Galveston, sending chunks of concrete hurtling toward the sky and twisting railcars in the vicinity. According to eyewitnesses, the blast originated from the rail dump area and spread through the fifteen-foot-long tunnel beneath, causing it to blast open.

Due to the blast, the north and south walls of the elevator's office building, as well as the the head house of the elevator, gave way, causing machinery to collapse, a storage silo to fall and the overhead conveyor system, which led from the elevator to the wharf, to crash down.

Other damages to the area included the destruction of four boxcars and an engine near the rail bin and the derailment of five other boxcars and another engine nearby. It was also noted that four parallel sets of tracks in the vicinity were twisted beyond repair for one hundred feet. The blast, which was heard nearly seventy miles away, caused damage not just to the wharf but to the city as well. In the city, windows all the way out to Broadway Street were shattered, and the electricity was knocked out along the waterfront and throughout downtown.

The cause of the blast was grain dust that ignited in the elevator's rail dump pit. Due to the economics of the period, ships were constantly being docked and unloaded, and then those ships were replaced by other ships, thus leaving no time to maintain the elevator. With all of the activity, there were massive levels of grain dust in the facility, and the rail dump yard had nearly zero visibility.

At least fifteen people were killed in the blast, and twenty-two others were injured and treated at John Sealy Hospital. Of the fifteen people killed, six of them were government officials who were there to inspect the operation.

5

HISTORIC STRUCTURES LOST TO OR DAMAGED BY FIRE

The Tremont Hotel
Twenty-Third and Postoffice Streets
January 12, 1865, Lost to Fire

Today's Tremont Hotel, although it carries the same name as the ones that came before, is far different from its predecessors. The earliest Tremont Hotel, which came into being in 1837, was a wood-frame dwelling built on the corner of Twenty-Third and Postoffice Streets that lasted only a short time before a strong gale struck the island and caused it to fall. The next structure to carry the name was built in 1839 by the firm of McKinney and Williams. This hotel, located at the southwest corner of Twenty-Third and Church Streets, would come to cover nearly an entire city block. At the time of its construction, it was an impressive structure, with long galleries on both floors stretching along its north and east façades, and it was the largest hotel in the state at the time.

On April 21, 1839, the hotel opened to the public with great fanfare and a lavish ball to commemorate the Battle of San Jacinto. Tickets to the event cost fifty dollars in Texas's currency of the time, or twenty-five dollars in gold. On January 15, 1840, the first public dinner to be held by the hotel was given in honor of General James Pinckney Henderson, the Republic of Texas's minister to France. The hotel played host to a number of presidents and other dignitaries on their visits to Galveston, as it was the premier place to stay while in Galveston. On April 19, 1861, while standing on a balcony on the north façade of the building, Sam Houston gave his final farewell address to a waiting crowd. Houston spoke of the dangers of seceding from the Union and that if they did, there would be "fires and rivers of blood." Texas did eventually secede from the Union, and the city and Port of Galveston were held captive by the Union throughout the Civil War. During the Civil War, the hotel was occupied by a large group of soldiers when a devastating fire struck the building.

On Friday, July 12, 1865, the Tremont Hotel, managed by Mr. Henry Howell Williams of Baltimore, had a fire erupt in its garret, causing flame and smoke to pour from beneath its shingles. A wind from the south caught the burning embers and began to sweep them along the block, dropping them onto the roofs of buildings nearby. Due to the combustible materials the hotel was made of and the scarcity of water with which to put it out, the flames burned unchecked and unabated throughout the building until the once-grand structure was nothing but a smoldering pile of ruin.

While there was much speculation as to what may have officially caused the fire, its true cause is still unknown.

After the destruction of the Tremont Hotel, a second hotel was built in 1872 on the same spot and in the same grand style. In 1928, the once grand structure met its fate when the wrecking ball destroyed it. It was not until 1986 that George and Cynthia Mitchell brought back the Tremont House name with a restoration and refurbishment of the old Leon and H. Blum Building and the old Belmont Hotel on Mechanic Street. Their vision repurposed these older buildings as a luxury hotel that was built in the same style as the original Tremont that once graced the fair city.

The Grand Southern Hotel
The Corner of Twenty-Second and Mechanic Streets
June 9, 1877, Lost to Fire

Samson Heidenheimer, a local Galveston merchant and auctioneer, hired local architect John Moser to design a four-story, forty-room Victorian hotel on the corner of Twenty-Second and Mechanic Streets. The hotel, which faced Twenty-Second Street, was a grand structure in the heart of the busy Galveston business district. Heidenheimer's hotel would later be known as

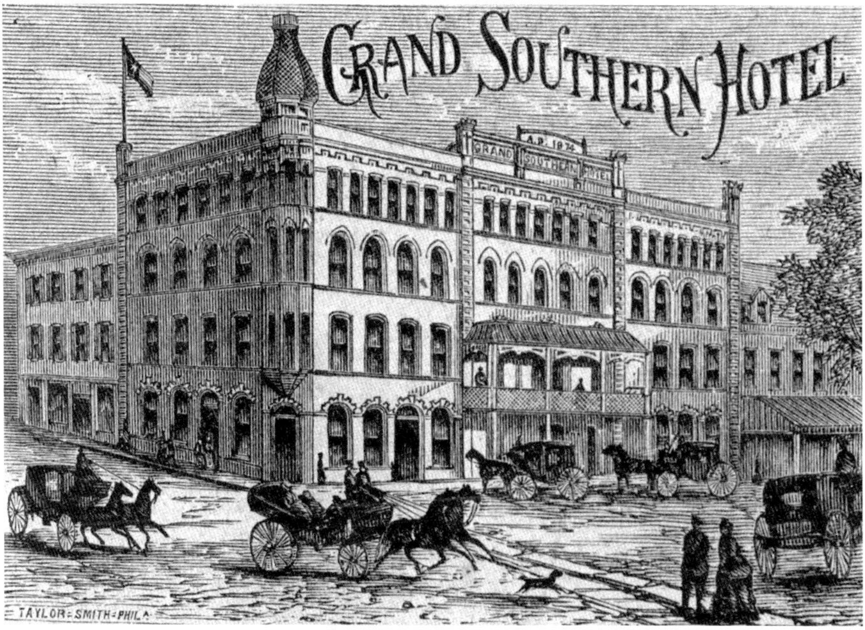

Grand Southern Hotel at the corner of Twenty-Second and Mechanic Streets. *Courtesy of Special Collections, Rosenberg Library, Galveston, Texas.*

the Grand Southern Hotel and would be a popular place to stay for visitors to Galveston.

An article in the *Galveston Daily News* from April 29, 1877, stated that the hotel had seen the construction of the new Tremont Hotel and wanted to "inaugurate a fair competition." With this in mind, the hotel was updated and remodeled. "The Southern is to be repainted inside, renovated, recarpeted; a gallery is to be put up along the Twenty-Second Street front, and a fresh start is to be taken. The dining room is to be enlarged, the kitchen is to be located differently and the most pleasant and inviting place of entertainment in the South is to be offered." By August 9, 1874, the hotel was nearly complete and ready to be occupied by Galveston's elite and incoming travelers.

The hotel lived up to its name and was one of the many warm and inviting establishments that were frequented by locals and visitors alike. Just short of being two years old, the grand hotel was lost in a fire that struck on June 9, 1877, and destroyed three blocks in the heart of Galveston's business district.

While tragedy had taken Heidenheimer's hotel, he was not ready to admit defeat. After the flames subsided and the debris was cleared away, Heidenheimer hired John Moser to design a three-story commercial building to stand in place of the old hotel. Over time, various businesses would call this building home, such as Herman Marwitz and Company, Heinrich and Mosel and Company and Fred F. Hunter Stationery. While this building was originally built by Heidenheimer, the building took the name of Fred F. Hunter when he moved his business to this location in 1923. He ran a business there continually for nearly fifty years before closing his doors in 1976. In 1984, the building underwent an intensive restoration, which restored the plaster façade and canopy to their original condition.

The Electric Pavilion
Twenty-First Street and Avenue Q
August 1, 1883, Lost to Fire

In 1880, Colonel William Henry Sinclair called on architect Nicholas J. Clayton to design a grand hall for the Sangerfest Festival, which had just been awarded to the city. A plot of land was purchased by Sinclair on the southeast corner of Twenty-First Street and Avenue Q. Construction bids were solicited at the end of January 1881, and by early February, the contract was awarded to Harry Devlin, who began work immediately on the great structure. By March 1881, the great steel arches were in place, and work continued at a rapid pace. The building eventually rose nearly three stories in height and had two large towers at its front, with a large auditorium to the rear of the building. Though the building was massive, through Clayton's use of wood veneered construction, it was given a delicate touch.

Early in April, the interior work was well underway when the electrical lighting equipment arrived from New Orleans. With the installation of the new electrical lighting, Devlin and his men could stretch their workday into the night and begin to work hard toward completing the building. Many wagers were placed that said the building would not be ready for the festival; however, by midnight on April 16, 1881, the interior was completed, and Sinclair toasted the workmen with champagne.

On April 17, 1881, a note was run in the *Galveston Daily News* that stated the brand-new pavilion that was being built for the Sangerfest Festival was nearly completed. "The interior of the building is finished, and the seats ready to set in position as soon as the floor is cleaned off." The pavilion, built by Colonel W.H. Sinclair of the Galveston City Railroad Company, was to be a grand structure with 5,800 seats for the thirteenth annual

Nicolas Clayton's Electric Pavilion, designed by William Sinclair for the 1881 Sangerfest. *Courtesy of Special Collections, Rosenberg Library, Galveston, Texas.*

Sangerfest Festival, which was to be held in the Oleander City from April 18 to April 22, 1881.

The festival, the most elaborate at the time, was extended for an impressive five days over its usual three, and it included two concerts. The festival started with an 8:00 p.m. reception of singers at the Union Depot, and they progressed by candlelight to the Artillery Hall, where they were addressed by the mayor and chairman of the reception committee. Over the course of the next several days, rehearsals commenced, with concerts in the evenings and oyster roasts and picnics each day. A grand ball was also held at the Garten Verein. The final day of the festival included an excursion on the bay followed by a reception and concert. Scores of people arrived for the festival, with Houston being represented for the first time by its Houston Maennerchor, a triple quartet.

As the festival ended, the pavilion took on a new role. It was converted into a casino by the Galveston City Railroad Company, and summertime concerts, dances and other events of interest were held there. In June 1882, Oscar Wilde gave his famous "Decorative Art" lecture at the pavilion. In the following month, the Texas Democratic State Convention was held at the pavilion as well.

The pavilion became a popular summer attraction, and many people came to see the various events or attractions hosted at this special venue. However, this beautiful structure would be quickly lost to flame, when, on August 1, 1883, at about 1:45 p.m., beachgoers noticed a small column of smoke rising from the south side of the pavilion. Shortly after, several flashes were noted before the flames appeared and began to climb up the building. At the sight of the flames, an alarm was sent to the fire department, which immediately raced to the scene. But due to the deplorable conditions of the road and the depth of the sand, movement was slow, and many precious moments passed before the first engine could arrive.

While most everyone escaped the fire, unbeknownst to others, a young man named Robert Spranger, the snare drum player for Professor Bob's Pavilion Band, had retired to the tower to lay his head down and rest after rehearsal. Robert awoke to smoke and flames. It didn't take long for him to realize his exit down the stairs was blocked by the flames. Upon that realization, he went to the window, where he tried to signal for help. Several times, he went to the window, and several times, he was told to jump for his life. The fires raged on, causing the building to become enveloped in a ball of flames. Finally, Robert realized that a rescue would not occur. He appeared once more in the window and then dove from the south tower. In the fall, his body twisted before he landed squarely on his back. In less than fifteen minutes, Spranger's life was extinguished due to the injuries he received.

Within a matter of hours, the entire building, which had been engulfed in flames, was completely burned out, leaving nothing but a pile of smoldering wood and ashes where the grand Electric Pavilion once stood.

Galveston Artillery Club
Corner of Twenty-Second & Market Streets
October 29, 1884, Lost to Fire

In 1840, a year after Galveston's incorporation, the city was home to approximately 1,200 residents. It was the entry point for scores of immigrants and a major coastal shipping port. Ongoing tensions between the young Republic of Texas and Mexico had led to the creation of several volunteer militia groups. On September 13, a group primarily composed of local businessmen and their clerks organized the Galveston Artillery Company.[19] The group received its charter in January 1841 to protect the harbor and the city. The group elected John Howe as captain, and he appointed A.C. Crawford, L.E. Nordman, W. Denny, C. Frankland and E.O. Lynch, as well as four sergeants and four corporals, as the company's first officers.

Locally, the company would participate in musters, drills and parades, as well as commemorations of the Battle of San Jacinto. However, the group was most well known for its lavish annual balls. Shortly after the Civil War and many reorganizations, in 1899, the group changed its name to the Galveston Artillery Club. This change marked that it was no longer a military organization; instead, it was more of a social organization.

The original Artillery Hall, built in 1875, served as a social club and armory for the Galveston Artillery Company. Prior to the construction of the Galveston Artillery Club at 902 Twenty-Second Street, the group met

Galveston's Artillery Hall at the corner of Twenty-Second and Winnie Streets, photographed by P.H. Rose, circa the 1880s. *Courtesy of the New York Public Library.*

at a hall located on the corner of Twenty-Second and Market Streets. On April 15, 1875, the Galveston Artillery Club purchased lots 1 and 2 of block 201 from George Ball for the construction of its new hall. When it was completed, the first floor of the wooden two-story structure served as an armory and drill room for the artillery company. The second floor served as a meeting room and grand hall for the company.

In 1893, the building was decommissioned and became known as the Galveston Artillery Club. On October 29, 1894, a fire started in the hall and consumed the building. Thankfully, the contents of the building had been saved, but the building was severely damaged. Undeterred, the members of the club rebuilt. Eventually, the members sold the building to the Central Christian Church, which kept the property until December 1921, when it decided to sell the property to the Gulf Refining Company. Today, the Galveston Artillery Club sits on the corner of Thirty-First Street and Avenue O, on property that was once a lavish estate known as Oakleigh.

Galveston County Courthouse
728 Church Street
December 16, 1896, Lost to Fire

Prior to the Civil War, around 1856 or 1857, the County of Galveston decided to build its courthouse in block 319, which was bounded by Winnie Avenue and Ball Avenue on its north and south side and Nineteenth and Twentieth Streets to the east and west. The original courthouse was situated at 728 Twentieth Street and was originally part of a compound that included the original Galveston County Jail and the gable-fronted courthouse.[20] The half block on which the courthouse sat was enclosed by a ten-foot-tall brick wall, which was used as a yard for the jail. The original jail was built on the Winnie Street side of the block, and the courthouse sat on the corner closest to Ball Avenue.

In 1875, Nicholas J. Clayton was awarded a contract to not only alter and remodel the building but also add a new vault to the county clerk's office. Around 1883, the original jailhouse was torn down, and a new jailhouse was built to replace it. Around the same time, the county court solicited bids for a remodeling of the old courthouse. Many were opposed to remodeling the structure and wanted a new building to replace the older one; yet the county commissioners decided that in order to save money, they needed to

Left: The original Galveston County Courthouse before the fire, photographed by P.H. Rose, circa the 1880s. *Courtesy of the New York Public Library.*

Below: The Galveston County Courthouse, Civil Appeals and Jail, circa 1880, after the remodel by Edward T. Heiner. *Author's collection.*

remodel the old building. Nicholas J. Clayton, Nathaniel Tobey and Eugene T. Heiner submitted bids for the contract; however, since Clayton's design had issues with moisture in the vaults, Heiner won the bid from him.

In 1881, Heiner began to resurface the courthouse and added a third story to the original two-story building. He also capped it with a tile mansard roof. In 1887, the building again saw improvements with the redesign of its plumbing system. Even with the remodeled building, there was a fear that the building was unsafe. This prompted the county to investigate the structure in an effort to find measures to strengthen it. For many years, there was talk of building a bigger and better structure, one in keeping with the progress and wealth of the city and the county. The commissioners were in favor of building a courthouse that would easily cost $500,000; however, opposition against the new courthouse caused the subject to finally be dropped in November 1895.

On Wednesday, December 16, a fire of unknown origin destroyed the courthouse. The fire was reported to the fire department at 11:15 p.m. from box 71. The fire first consumed the slate roof on the east end of the building. While firemen sprayed the roof, the flames burned beneath the roof, destroying its supports and causing it to collapse. The fire then began burning downward, through the iron support beams of the structure. It is believed the steel vaults were still secure and saved most of the county records, many of which date back to 1839. By 2:00 a.m., the fire had been contained. Even though the roof had caved in, the four walls remained standing; the first and second floors were found to still be in good condition, and the vaults indeed remained intact. On April 21, 1899, a new county courthouse replaced the structure that had burned in the earlier fire.

The Beach Hotel
Beach Street, Between Twenty-Third and Twenty-Fourth Streets
July 23, 1898, Lost to Fire

In 1882, Colonel William H. Sinclair of the Galveston City Railroad Company led a plan to develop Galveston's beachside as a premier resort destination. With the previous construction of Galveston's Electric Pavilion, Sinclair wanted to complement it with a grand hotel known as the Beach Hotel.[21] Initially, Colonel Sinclair had estimated that the construction would cost only $50,000; however, shortly after the $50,000 was reached, he once again launched an ambitious campaign to acquire another $50,000 to build the most premier resort in the country. While it seemed like the second $50,000 goal would never be achieved, a substantial investment from the Gulf, Colorado and Santa Fe Railroad assisted in achieving his goal.

A site was chosen in the southeast corner of block 117, and by January 1883, construction had begun on the enormous structure, planned to be 243 feet long and 112 feet wide. To support this type of structure on Galveston's beachfront, the hotel would need a substantial base on which to stand. Massive cedar pilings were drilled deep into the earth, while the tops stood an impressive 18 feet above the ground.

As construction progressed, electric lights were installed in the building to allow for construction to continue throughout the night. It was hoped that the hotel would be ready for the 1883 summer season. By April, the exterior of the hotel was completed, and work continued on the interior. By the time the hotel was completed, it had three floors of public space containing 119 guest rooms, a large dining room on the second floor, a billiard hall and bar beneath a full attic that contained tanks for the salt and freshwater systems of the hotel. Crowning the hotel was a large dome that housed the tank and machine that operated the hotel's impressive hydraulic elevator.

On its exterior, the hotel was surrounded by verandas, which allowed guests and visitors alike to stroll along its exterior or just sit and enjoy the sound of the waves as they splashed nearby. The exterior of the building

Clayton's Grand Beach Hotel built for the Galveston Electric Railway. *Author's collection.*

was painted mauve with a hint of golden-green, and the impressive roof was painted a bold red with white stripes. In front of the hotel, a bandstand was built, which allowed guests to listen to the music from the verandas. Also, in the area directly in front of the hotel was the Pagoda Bathhouse and several small lunch and curio stands.

J. Harvey Pierce of New York leased the hotel from the Beach Hotel and Seaside Improvement Company and held an impressive grand opening on July 4, 1883. The hotel got off to a great start, allowing guests to enjoy the island and the beach. However, the tourism industry in Galveston was cyclical, and the hotel did suffer when it was low.

In the late 1880s, Colonel Sinclair was working with Minneapolis investors who were interested in the hotel; however, the hotel failed to sell. In 1890, Nicholas Clayton once again came in to rebuild the smokestack that had collapsed the year before. By the spring of 1894, the Galveston City Railroad Company had begun to talk about enlarging the hotel; however, by the end of the year, the hotel was auctioned off to J.P. Alvey so the bondholders could be paid back their original investment.

In 1895, the hotel once again reopened, but it was at this moment that Colonel Sinclair chose to sell his holdings in the Beach Hotel and Seaside Improvement Company and the Galveston City Railroad Company. The City of Galveston acquired the property due to a lien of $15,000 against it. As the city began to assess its investment, the true nature of what it had acquired began to reveal itself. The structure itself had begun to deteriorate so badly that it was declared to be a fire hazard, and insurers were warned it would be a great risk. It was also learned that since 1887, the Beach Hotel and Seaside Improvement Company had paid no city, state or school district taxes.

In March 1896, the hotel was sold to W.E. Hughes of Dallas, who owned and operated Galveston's Tremont Hotel and Dallas's Grand Windsor Hotel. Mr. Hughes hired Nicholas Clayton to come in, renovate and repaint the grand structure. A report by the *Galveston Daily News* on May 4, 1896, stated, "Gingerbread on the big Beach Hotel has been frosted; zebra stripes of brilliant carmine, olive and extra pale green encircle the spectacular dome and crawl all over the galleried structure."

Once again, the hotel opened for business, and things began to look good for a while. But in 1898, when a sewage pipe that carried waste from the hotel to the Gulf of Mexico was to be replaced, the city health officer declared that a more sanitary disposal system needed to be installed. At that time, two large groups, the Texas State Bar Association and the Texas

The remains of the Beach Hotel foundation in the surf after the 1900 storm. *Author's collection.*

Democratic Party, were both scheduled to convene in Galveston, so the manager threatened not to open the hotel if the pipe couldn't be replaced. Finally, a compromise was reached.

It was around this time that a night watchman discovered a small fire near the unused boiler room and the watchdogs were stolen from the property. On July 22, 1898, the hotel reopened for business, but business was soon brought to a screeching halt. The next day, on July 23, a fire began in the service wing of the hotel, and flames leapt through the wooden structure. As the fire gained intensity, a strong northerly wind threatened to spread it to nearby structures. Realizing that the hotel could not be saved, the firefighters focused their efforts on trying to save the surrounding structures.

Wilbur Goodman was interviewed by Robert Nesbitt and was quoted as saying:

> *I remember very well the night the beautiful old wooden Beach Hotel burned to the ground. That was sometime in the spring of 1898, and I was about eleven years of age at the time, and—as is common with most*

young boys—I was excited, interested in fires. I remember being awakened by the fire whistle on the waterworks, at Thirtieth and Avenue H, four blocks from our home. We could tell by the way the whistle sounded where the fire was located. One blast. Silence. Three short blasts. Silence. Five short blasts. Silence. Then repeat it all over. That meant fire box 135. I looked out the bay window of my bedroom, toward the south and saw the light from the fire.

I thought it must be the Ursuline Academy. I never missed a fire—day or night—if I could help it. So, I quickly pulled on my clothes, didn't stop to put on my shoes and told my mother and father sleeping in the next room where I was headed.

When I got near the Ursuline Academy, I could see the fire was farther out. So, I raced toward the beach and saw the Beach Hotel at Twenty-Third and Beach in complete flames. Guests had begun to get away from the hotel when I arrived and were still in their night clothes, walking away from the intense heat.

The flames were so hot the firemen could not get close enough to throw water on the blaze, and we all had to stand around and watch the fine old wooden structure burn to the ground. It was a real sad scene—Galveston's first great beachfront hotel and tourist attraction and a really beautiful building by Clayton, which everyone admired.[22]

Seaside Hotel
2021 Tremont Street
December 9, 1917, Lost to Fire

In the early 1900s, with the development of the automobile, people were able to travel with much more ease than they had on trains and boats. And with Galveston's renewed vigor to take its place as the premier vacation destination, hotels bought into that ideal by building hotels close to the beaches, which allowed vacationers to enjoy their stays with as much ease as possible. These hotels included Galveston's Seaside Hotel, which was situated on the northwest corner of Twenty-Third Street and Avenue Q at 2021 Tremont Street, and the nearby Gulf View Hotel, which had twenty-eight rooms.

On March 11, 1907, the Seaside Hotel Company purchased lot 8 and half of lot 9 in the southeast block of out-lot 92 to build a frame building for a hotel at a cost of $12,600. A *Galveston Daily News* article from April 28,

The Seaside Hotel. *Courtesy of Special Collections, Rosenberg Library, Galveston, Texas.*

1907, reported that the new hotel was "nearing completion….Practically all the outside work has been completed, and a large force of carpenters are now engaged on the interior work. Painters, plumbers and electricians are all at work, and it is probable that about thirty-five or forty men are employed about the building."

The Seaside Hotel, which opened on May 25, 1907, boasted seventy-seven rooms close to the beach, allowing visitors to enjoy nearby accommodations after a long day outside. W.H. Rickert's Drugstore was located on the northwest corner of the ground floor as well as Stroberg's Restaurant.

On Saturday, December 9, 1917, a fire of unknown origins started on second floor of the hotel. An alarm was sounded at 3:28 a.m. As the fire department rushed to the hotel to try to extinguish the flames, the heavy northwest wind kept spreading the flames. They reached across Avenue Q and began burning the Crystal Palace Hotel and the Snug Harbor Hotel. All eight fire companies arrived on the scene, and with their quick and efficient work, they were able to get the fire in check and prevent any further damage to the Crystal Palace and Snug Harbor Hotels.

By 5:30 a.m., the fire was out, and the true damage was finally seen. The Seaside Hotel and the Gulf View Hotel next door were total losses. During an inspection later that afternoon, around about 2:00 p.m., Policeman William Alexander discovered the burned body of a soldier among the ruins. Little was known about the soldier other than that he checked in on Friday night and was about twenty-five years of age and five foot, six inches in height. When the fire started, Mrs. Levy, who was in charge of the hotel, called each room to warn the inhabitants of the fire. Several times, she called and rapped on the soldier's door. Receiving no response, she escaped the burning building after being told by the other guests that everyone had left.

Total loss of the Seaside Hotel, the Gulf View Hotel and the restaurant and drugstore cost about $80,000.

Hall Home/Mottexas/Dana Place
Galveston Island, West End
December 27, 1925, Lost to Fire

Warren Dewitt Clinton Hall was born in 1794 in Union County, South Carolina. At an early age, he and his family moved to Louisiana, where he grew up and received his education. He went on to study law in Natchitoches and later joined the Mexican Republican Army of the North in 1812. In 1813, Hall resigned his post and returned to Louisiana, where he protested against the butchery of the royalist prisoners held in Alazan Heights.[23]

In November 1814, Hall joined a company of Louisiana volunteers in the defense of New Orleans against the British during the War of 1812. After the war, in 1816–17, he participated in several filibustering expeditions, including one that brought him to Galveston Island during its occupation by Francisco Xavier Mina and General Louis-Michel Aury. Hall supported the revolutionary movement headed by James Long and were believed to have befriended Jean Laffite, who took over the island. Although he befriended Laffite, Warren D.C. Hall took no part in the questionable activities of the buccaneer.

In 1821, on land far out on the West End, close to the current-day Stewart Mansion, Hall built his home, which he lived in for a number of years before moving to Brazoria with his wife.[24] After Hall's departure from Galveston, his property had a number of owners, including Isadore Dyer and William R. Smith, until it was purchased in 1878 by Marcus Fulton Mott. For many years, Elmer E. Dana leased the place, and the home became known as the "Dana Place." Colonel Mott's daughter Lillian Cash inherited the property

Nicholas Clayton's original Harmony Hall. *Author's collection.*

from her father upon his death and was occupying it at the time of the fire that destroyed the landmark.

Harmony Hall
2128 Church Street
February 5, 1928, Lost to Fire

The idea for Galveston's Harmony Hall began with the Harmony Club, Galveston's social elite of the Jewish community. Early in 1881, several wealthy members of the club went to Clayton and commissioned him to build a grand meetinghouse. Clayton immediately went to work on his commission, and in May 1881, he exhibited his plans for the new hall.

A site, located at 2128 Church Street, was purchased, and an earlier structure, the Ryland Chapel, Galveston's first Methodist church building, as well as other buildings that were on the site, were moved in July 1881. In June 1882, a construction contract for $47,000 was awarded to Henry Devlin, and construction commenced. Construction on the great hall lasted a little over a year, and the building was completed in August 1883.

Harmony Hall, destroyed by fire. *Courtesy of Special Collections, Rosenberg Library, Galveston, Texas.*

On September 1, 1883, the building opened, and the Harmony Club moved in. The club enjoyed the building for nearly twelve years before it realized it couldn't really afford the massive structure, as its investors could not redeem their bonds. So, in 1895, the club moved to a more modest structure that had also been built by Clayton on Postoffice Street, and the original building was sold to the Galveston Business University. While it was owned by the school, the building suffered major damage from the 1900 hurricane, and it received repairs from Clayton thereafter. In 1902, the school decided to sell the property, and Galveston's Scottish Rite Temple purchased it.

On the evening of February 5, 1928, while several members of the Scottish Rite Temple were playing billiards on the first floor, a faulty wire in an organ on the upper floor caused a fire that began to engulf the building. Unknown to the members below, the flames began to rapidly consume the building. An alarm was sounded by spectators on the street, and firefighters rushed to the scene. As the firefighters entered the building to combat the flames, the surprised members soon learned exactly what was happening.

With lightning speed, the members and firefighters helped remove the valuable furnishings from the building, rescuing as much as possible. Meanwhile, firefighters outside sprayed the building and tried to combat the flames. Soon, no one was allowed back into the building, and the fire was eventually contained after several long hours of fighting. Many valuable and irreplaceable sacred objects were lost in the fire; however, much was also saved.

After the blaze, the rubble was cleared from the corner of Church and Twenty-Third Streets, and a new Scottish Rite Temple rose on the site where Nicholas Clayton's Harmony Hall had stood. One of the features incorporated into the new structure was the original marble staircase from the earlier structure.

William A. Guyton Home
Northeast Corner of Fifty-Third Street and Avenue S
June 8, 1913, Lost to Fire

In 1909, William A. Guyton and his wife, Margaret, purchased property on the northeast side of Fifty Third Street at Avenue S, where they would raise their family. The home was a two-story residence with basement. After purchasing the property, the couple remodeled and improved the home, making it one of the most beautiful two-story residences on Galveston's West End.

William A. Guyton and family, circa 1911. *Courtesy of the descendants of William A. Guyton.*

William A. Guyton's home in flames, billowing smoke. *Author's collection.*

William A. Guyton's home, gone after the fire. *Author's collection.*

Shortly after 6:00 a.m. on Sunday, June 8, 1913, a fire of unknown origins was discovered at the Guytons' home. On the day of the fire, William was out of town on business; however, his wife and six children were there. Margaret, who had been seriously ill for several days, was unable to leave her bed, so she was carried from her home to the home of Robert S. Smith, on the northeast corner of Fifty-Fourth Street and Avenue S, where the family was temporarily sheltered.

It was believed that the fire had been started by a defective flue or faulty wiring in the kitchen. When the fire department appeared on the scene, the home was already ablaze. Immediately, the fire department went to work trying to put out the fire while also removing valuable furnishings, including a piano, from the home to save them from the fire.

As the fire department fought the blaze, several hundred men from nearby Fort Crockett rushed to assist in trying to save the home and its furnishings. Two firemen received burns to their faces and necks when a portion of a burning wall fell on them. Both firemen were rushed to John Sealy Hospital, where they received medical attention. Meanwhile, two soldiers were also injured and taken to Fort Crockett, where they received care from the base.

Trube Building
121 Market Street
November 6, 1945

On July 10, 1875, an article ran in the *Galveston Daily News* that said Mr. John Clement Trube was building a new two-story brick building on Market Street, between the Galveston Daily News building and the old bank. By October, the building was open for occupancy, and E.S. Levy and Company was moving in with a portion of its clothing store. Over time, the building increased in size, and by 1927, it was three stories tall.

On December 20, 1909, the building received its first of three fire threats when a blaze broke out on the second story. It seems the fire originated in the candy kitchen of George Theophilakes when one of the workers, who was boiling candy on the stove, stepped away for a brief moment to light another stove—the candy boiled over, igniting immediately.

At 2:41 p.m., reports of the blaze were sent to the fire department via the call box, and the fire department hurried to the scene as quickly as possible. Within moments, about twelve to fourteen streams of water were sprayed on

Scottish Rite Parade on Market Street, circa 1910–20. The Trube Building is located in the middle-right of the image. *Author's collection.*

the fire, and the hoses were stretched across Market and Tremont Streets, causing traffic to back up for nearly an hour.

After the fire, it was determined the fire caused between $50,000 and $90,000 worth of damage. And even though the fire was contained, it did cause some damage to Flatto's Shoe Store, Sam J. Williams Clothing Store, New York Dental Parlor's and Artcraft Photography Studio. While the fire was mostly contained to the Trube Building, due to the water, the Purdy Bookstore, located on the first floor of the building next door, the Rosenberg Bank Building, did sustain about $1,000 worth of damage, which was covered by insurance.

In the early morning hours on January 23, 1930, an automatic sterilization machine in the dental office of Dr. W.L. James failed to operate properly, shorted and caught fire. Smoke was noticed pouring from the building at 3:50 a.m., and by the time the fire was discovered, it had already destroyed the automatic sterilizer and was spreading to other parts of the office. The fire department sprayed water on the fire and quickly got it under control. The estimated cost of damages from the fire was about $500.

Sadly, on the morning of November 6, 1945, a fire once again broke out in the Trube Building, this time causing so much damage that the building couldn't be saved. The fire began in the back of Mr. Levin's Army and Navy Store at 2215 Market Street sometime before 5:00 a.m., and it quickly progressed from a two-alarm fire to a general alarm, causing over one hundred firefighters to rush to the scene.

Within an hour and a half of the discovery of the fire, the blaze was brought under control by the fire company and quickly extinguished by numerous jets of water. Since the fire had gutted the bottom floor, the upper floor began to collapse. The heat from the fire began to affect the power lines behind the building, which began to pop and eventually fall to the ground below.

When the fire was finally extinguished, Baxter & Wilson's Clothing Store sustained about $17,500 worth of damages, as it owned nearly one-third of the building—nearly $15,000 worth of the damages covered the contents of the store. Other businesses that were damaged in the fire were Luby's Cafeteria, with $35,000 in damages; Levin's Army and Navy Store, with $50,000 in damages; Morris Photography Studio, with $7,500 in damages; and Henry's Book Store, with $5,000 in damages. Damages to the Trube Building itself were estimated to cost $20,000.

On March 15, 1946, the Trube Building, which once stood gracefully on the 2200 block of Market Street, was torn down and replaced by a two-story building.

The Balinese Room
2107 Seawall
October 3, 1954, Gutted by Fire, Rebuilt; Destroyed by Hurricane Ike, 2008

In 1942, the historic Balinese Room would make its appearance on Galveston's entertainment scene as the crown jewel of the Maceo empire. However, this historic pier, which jutted six hundred feet into the Gulf of Mexico, had been there since the 1920s—it was just known under a different name. In 1923, the pier was first opened as the Chop Suey, which was closed in 1932 for an illegal gambling violation. In 1936, the pier was reopened, this time under a new name, Sui Jen, and with new looks. While business did well at this time, with the onset of World War II, Asian-themed locales tended to be less favored.

Salvatore "Sam" Maceo began a complete remodel of the Sui Jen to give it more of a South Seas motif. He also completely renamed the club. It would reopen as the Balinese Room in 1942 and delight guests of the pier with live music and shows from well-known entertainers, such as Phil

The Chop Suey Cafe, Opposite Hotel Galvez, Galveston, Texas.

The original Maceo-owned pier, Chop Suey interior before it was transformed into the Balinese Room, circa the 1930s. *Author's collection.*

Harris, Alice Faye, Bob Hope and others, during its heyday. On April 16, 1951, in Baltimore, at John Hopkins Hospital, Salvatore "Sam" Maceo passed away, leaving the Maceo empire to his brother Rosario "Rose" Maceo and his nephews Anthony and Victor Fertitta. On March 15, 1954, Rose Maceo passed, and full ownership of the empire reverted to Anthony and Victor Fertitta.

On Sunday, October 3, 1954, at about 4:15 a.m., a fire broke out in the light control booth of the famed Balinese Room. The fire was discovered by a porter, who quickly reported the blaze to the fire department. Upon their arrival, the firemen worked quickly, connecting their fire hose to the only hydrant, which was located two hundred feet away. In the meantime, the drapes of the Balinese Room caught fire, and the blaze began to roar. The fire burned a hole in the roof of the building, sending flames shooting nearly two hundred feet over the gulf.

As the flames roared, the pier was consumed; the nearby Dreamland Café was nearly set aflame by the debris and sparks being cast off from the burning Balinese Room. By noon, the fire had been brought under control, although the pier still smoldered. All day Sunday, firemen were stationed at the seawall, fire hoses at the ready, just in case the fire reignited. After the fire, it was learned that nine trunks of costumes belonging to entertainer Sophie

The restored Balinese Room, circa the 1980s. *Author's collection.*

Tucker, several costumes and musical instruments belonging to comedian Fran Warren and the special music library of Bob Cross and his orchestra were destroyed in the flames. It was estimated that the damages to these items cost nearly $200,000.

While the Balinese Room did rebuild and reopen, it was only open for a short time. On May 30, 1957, the famous club was raided by the Texas Rangers, and its glory days were finally over. The club was officially shut down in 1961. That same year, Hurricane Carla came ashore and caused tremendous damage to the pier, washing away several supporting beams and causing it to sag and deteriorate.

In 2002, the famed Balinese Room would once again come to life, as its doors were opened for a short time. Sadly, its life was short-lived. On September 13, 2008, as Hurricane Ike roared across Galveston, the pier collapsed, and the last remaining vestiges of the storied pier were strewn about the gulf and across the island.

Today, a small pergola structure now stands on the seawall, marking the former site of the famed Balinese Room.

St. Mary's Orphanage before it became Galveston College. *Author's collection.*

St. Mary's Orphanage
4015 Avenue Q
February 11, 1960, Damaged in a Fire

On September 8, 1900, a category 4 hurricane came ashore in Galveston, decimating the island. One of the main buildings damaged in the storm was St. Mary's Orphan Asylum, located at present-day Sixty-Ninth and Seawall Streets. This complex, which consisted of three buildings, housed ninety-three children and ten nuns. After the storm passed, all vestiges of the buildings were gone, and all but three of the ninety-three orphans had died in the storm.

In 1901, a wood-frame building located at Fortieth Street and Avenue Q was purchased, and the orphanage was moved there. In 1950, a large three-story brick structure with basement was built to replace the aging wooden structure.

On Thursday, February 11, 1960, at about 6:15 a.m., a fire broke out at St. Mary's Orphanage at 4015 Avenue Q. The fire started in the vestry behind the altar while a mass was taking place. All twenty-one children and faculty members escaped the building unharmed. It was believed that the fire started when a careless altar boy dropped a match while preparing for mass.

Due to the fire, the walls were badly scorched, and the interior ceiling was open, exposing the piping and wiring in the ceiling. Also, the furniture in the room was severely burned, and the altar vessels were blackened due to the flames. The damage was repaired by the orphanage, and daily operations continued as normal.

The orphanage remained at this location until August 2, 1967, when the building was deeded to Galveston College, which now runs the site. The original orphanage was the only building on the property until other structures were added by the college.

Masonic Hall
2027 Postoffice Street
January 13, 1966, Lost to Fire

In 1839, Harmony Lodge No. 6 A.F. and A.M. formed in Galveston, and it was formally chartered in January 1840. In 1848, land was purchased on the corner of Twenty-First and Postoffice Streets for the erection of a temple. On January 25, 1856, the cornerstone for the new proposed $100,000 temple was laid at the annual session of the Grand Lodge of Texas in Galveston. Presiding over the ceremony was Grand Master Ebenezer B. Nichols.

Due to the onset of the Civil War, the cornerstone laid quietly on the lot without any construction. Attempts to continue with construction were met with failure, and slowly, the stone was covered with earth until it was once again uncovered on December 14, 1882. On December 27, 1882, Deputy Grand Master William H. Nichols, the son of Grand Master Ebenezer Nichols, presided over the second laying of the cornerstone, using the original stone from 1856.

On April 17, 1884, a formal dedication of the new temple was held, and former grand master Marcus Fulton Mott addressed those assembled for the annual convocation of the Grand Commandery of the Knights Templar of the State of Texas.

The building, designed by Nicholas Clayton, was built at a cost of $57,000, and it was owned by several Masonic bodies in Galveston. It was governed by a board of directors that represented the lodges. The original three-story structure was built in the Italian Neo-Gothic style, with a tower that rose 120 feet above the ground on its northwest corner. During the

Galveston's Masonic Lodge, located on the corner of Postoffice and Twenty-First Streets and designed by Nicholas Clayton. *Author's collection.*

1900 hurricane, the tower collapsed, and much of the original façade of the north and west walls was damaged. Shortly after the storm, the building was restored, but in the 1915 hurricane, it was damaged again, and it was then that much of the renaissance details were removed from the building. Throughout the 1920s, the structure was struck by a number of fires.

At midnight on January 13, 1942, a disastrous fire erupted from the ABC Racket Store and the lodge. Firemen broke through the windows of the business below in order to get to the flames. Two firemen, Henry Reagan and Vernon Oldham, were injured by the shattered glass; however, after being treated at John Sealy Hospital, the two were released. The firemen fought valiantly for nearly five hours before the fire was brought under control at 2:00 a.m. The damage was mostly contained to the second floor, which housed the Masonic hall. The damage to the building and its fixtures and furniture was estimated to cost about $100,000. Additional damage to the store below brought the damage estimates to about $150,000.

After the fire, the foundation and lower floors were restored, and in February 1954, the Masonic body moved from the hall to the old Temple B'Nai Israel Synagogue, which it purchased for $80,000. After the Masonic body moved from the hall, the building was leased out the ABC Racket Store. On January 13, 1966, the remaining portion of the historic building was lost when the ABC Racket Store burned due to arson.

It should be noted that this building housed the first circulating library in Texas, the forerunner of today's Rosenberg Library. It is also in this historic structure where the artillery club was first organized.

Galveston Cotton and Woolen Mills
Winnie Street
October 24, 1969, Lost Due to Fire

On August 23, 1890, with a capital of $500,000, the Galveston Cotton and Woolen Mill, the largest manufacturing plant in the city, was established on the north side of Winnie Street, between Fortieth and Forty-First Streets. The Providence, Rhode Island engineering firm of C.R. Makepeace and Company completed the construction of the building, a magnificent four-story structure with two five-story towers that fronted Winnie Street. Also on the property was a 150-foot-tall smokestack that served the structure. It was the second-largest smokestack on the island at that time.

Galveston Cotton and Woolen Mill, circa 1894. *Courtesy of Special Collections, Rosenberg Library, Galveston, Texas.*

Seaboard Rice and Milling Company, old Galveston Cotton and Woolen Mill, circa 1918. *Author's collection.*

The business provided employment for 650 textile workers, many of whom lived in company housing that was built on block 342, bounded by Forty-Second and Forty-Third Streets and Avenues G and H. On this property were fourteen one-story houses that fronted Avenues G and H.

In 1898, the structure was sold for $325,000 at a trustee's sale to John H. Sealy, who planned to continue the mill's operations; however, by 1900, the building was no longer operating and was again up for sale. In 1902, the building was sold the Seaboard Rice and Milling Company, which owned the building until 1928, when it was sold to the Galveston Rice Milling Company. In 1932, the Galveston Rice Milling Company closed, and the building was once again sold. It went through several owners, including the Cotton Pickery, before finally closing for good.

On Friday, October 24, 1969, the old Galveston Cotton and Woolen Mill, which had been slated for demolition, was slowly being dismantled when the structure was consumed in flames. The fire was started by sparks from a nearby housing project, where a bucket of hot tar was accidentally spilled on a roof. High winds carried the sparks from the housing complex and dropped them on the abandoned structure, igniting the old-growth pine timbers.

At about 5:30 p.m., the ancient wooden structure was consumed by the blaze, with flames shooting 150 feet into the air. The fire department had just returned from the housing complex fire when an alarm was received for the abandoned mill. The fire department raced to the scene and began to wet buildings in the area to keep them from catching fire. By about 9:30 p.m., the massive structure was a smoldering pile—and it would smolder for some time.

Sydnor-Heidenheimer Castle
1602 Sealy Street
November 1973, Damaged in a Fire

Heidenheimer's Castle was originally built in 1857 for then Galveston mayor John Seabrook Sydnor. Sydnor was a successful businessman and had several business interests, including railroads, commission businesses and real estate businesses. He was instrumental in constructing a brick wharf. He was a strong advocate for schools and fire and police departments for his beloved Galveston.

His previous home, the Powhatan Hotel, was built in 1847 on Twenty-First Street, between Avenues M and N. The hotel was built entirely of

Looking down Sealy Street, showing Heidenheimer's Castle with the tower in the middle, circa 1907. *Author's collection.*

lumber in the grand Greek Revival style, which was popular at the time. The home, created in Maine, was shipped to the island and reassembled on its new site. Due to its location away from the main commercial district, the hotel wasn't frequented often—even though a horse-drawn omnibus offered visitors direct access to the commercial district.

Sydnor built his new castle using "tabby," or concrete made with lime created by burning oyster shells. This lime would then be mixed with water, sand, ash and more broken oyster shells to make the tabby concrete. The home, when constructed, was a typical Greek Revival structure of the time, with a central hallway flanked by two rooms on each side, both upstairs and down.

In 1869, while visiting his son in Lynchburg, Sydnor passed away and left his son in charge of his home and estate. Shortly after his father's death, Sydnor's son sold the home to Barnabas T. Loring of Boston, Massachusetts, for $7,000. Loring would keep the home for about ten years before selling the property again in 1884, this time to Samson Heidenheimer for $2,500.

Starting in 1885, Heidenheimer altered the house by adding a new wing to the back, a tower to the front and several more porches. After the nearly $20,000 remodel, the home boasted thirty-seven rooms and had earned the nickname "Heidenheimer's Castle." In March 1890, Heidenheimer constructed a conservatory for the home, but unfortunately, on February 22, 1891, Heidenheimer passed away due to complications from surgery.

In Heidenheimer's will, he left the house and the bulk of his estate to his wife; however, his children would take her to court and take the house from her. Heidenheimer's children took possession of the home until 1936, when it was sold to William J.N. Hammons for $2,500. After Hammons,

South view *(front side)*, circa 1967. *Courtesy of the Library of Congress.*

the house was owned by several people, until Charlotte Warner purchased it, determined to bring it back to its original splendor. Charlotte and her husband, Kenneth, purchased the home in 1962 and immediately began restoring it. In 1968, Charlotte's beloved Kenneth passed away, and maintaining and caring for the home became a huge undertaking for her.

In November 1973, the police received a report that vandals were stealing valuables from the home. Charlotte was not home at the time, as she was recovering from surgery at John Sealy Hospital. A few hours later, a fire

West and south side, circa 1967. *Courtesy of the Library of Congress.*

engulfed the home. Firefighters rushed to the scene and did their best to put the flames out, but by the time the fire was out, the building itself was heavily damaged, along with most of its contents.

In May 1974, Charlotte sold the home with the intention that that next owner would restore it; however, the next owner was transferred before work could even begin. Eventually, an estate auction was held, and many pieces of furniture were sold from the home. In October 1974, the house was sold for $17,500, and it was soon dismantled. Luckily, some of the architectural elements were salvaged from the home. But sadly, the last vestiges of the home were removed in 1975. Today, two homes that match the architectural style of the neighborhood fill the lot that once held the grand home.

Reisner Building, the location of the Old Central Hotel, circa 1966. *Courtesy of Special Collections, Rosenberg Library, Galveston, Texas.*

Central Hotel/Stella Maris Apartments
2400 Block of Market Street
April 20, 1977, Lost Due to Fire

On September 29, 1870, the *Galveston Daily News* ran on article on page 3 about the origins of the Central Hotel. It stated that the hotel was built by Judge John L. Darragh and that Mrs. L.B. White was its proprietor. The new Central Hotel was centrally located and was a convenient distance from the business district.

The hotel started its life in 1870 as the Central Hotel, and it would retain its name until 1900, when it was renamed Avenue House Hotel. It kept this name until May 1976, when the property was purchased and renamed the Stella Maris Apartments.

On April 20, 1977, a fire broke out at the base of the stairwell of the old hotel and engulfed the building, quickly destroying it. The evening prior, forty-seven people were listed as having been in the building; however, only thirty-eight could be accounted for after the fire. Firefighters fought the intense blaze for a few hours before finally bringing it under control.

Reports showed that the fire began on the second floor of the building, around the staircase. It seems that an arsonist had dumped accelerant, which several residents noticed just before the fire occurred. However, when the fire started, many found themselves to be trapped in the building, as their windows were nailed shut and their only exits were blocked by fire. Several chose to jump from the windows or scale the building to escape the fire.

In the aftermath, volunteers combed through the rubble for days to search for survivors or victims of the fire. Daily, the numbers seemed to contradict each other; over time, the death toll would rise to twenty.

Nearly seven years later, a case against Johns Management and Isle Management, which owned and operated the hotel, was brought to court. After several hours of deliberation, the companies were found responsible for the obstruction of the third-floor fire escape, the failure to install a sprinkler system or fire doors in the building and the failure to maintain exit lights, smoke detectors or fire alarms.

In the aftermath, the City of Galveston looked at itself and its fire department and found that they had fallen short of their promise to serve and protect the citizens of the city. City Ordinance 78-15 stated that the fire department was to maintain 117 members in its fire suppression unit;

however, at the time of the fire, it had only 107. Since that time, the ordinance has been met, and the fire department continually looks for ways to improve on its promise to protect citizens from the threat of fire.

Ufford Building
Corner of Mechanic and Twenty-Third Streets
February 2, 1978, Destroyed by Fire

On this site, block 563, lot 1, at the corner of Mechanic and Twenty-Third Streets, in 1860, E.L. Ufford hired John Brown to construct a new iron-fronted, fireproof building to replace his earlier building, which had collapsed in 1859. The new Greek Revival building was simple in design and contained a small cornerstone on the northeast corner of the second floor, which read "E.L.U. 1860."

After the construction of the building was complete, numerous businesses took up residence. In 1907, the building was leased by Charles L. Beissner and renamed the Palmetto Hotel. Beissner later sold out to the International and Great Northern Railroad, which converted the building into a freight and ticket office. In 1910, the third floor of the building was leased to Charles H. Moore, who used it as a boardinghouse. In 1919, Mrs. Ella Jordan became the proprietor of the Palmetto Hotel. Over time, various businesses moved in and out of the building—until about 1975, when the building was bought by the First Hutchings–Sealy National Bank. After purchasing the building, the bank planned to tear it down to make room for a parking lot. Peter Brink and the Galveston Historical Foundation fought with an injunction to try to save this historic structure.

With the injunction in place, it was noted by Brink that the door was jimmied open and standing ajar with the fire escape down. Due to the recent rash of fires in the area, it was Brink's hope that the building would be locked up and secured against anyone who might want to go in and out of the building at their leisure. A clerk at the Belmont Hotel across the street from the Ufford Building noticed several vagrants climbing the fire escape and entering the building on various occasions. And an eyewitness stated that they had noticed several homeless people entering the building on Wednesday, the day before the fire.

Around noon on Thursday, Officer George Riveaux saw and smelled smoke coming from the vacant Ufford Building and reported it to the

Firemen fighting the fire at the Ufford Building, located on the corner of Mechanic and Twenty-Third Streets. *Author's collection.*

Remains of the Ufford Building after the fire. *Courtesy of Richard Eisenhour.*

fire department. He then began a sweep of the building to look for any occupants; however, he found none.

Firemen arrived on the scene and could see nothing but smoke billowing from the building. Within an hour, the flames had already engulfed the building and burst through the roof, causing it to collapse. Thankfully, although the fire was an intense one, it never spread to any nearby structures. But the Ufford Building was destroyed. Today, the former location of this building serves as a private parking lot.

1880 Garten Verein Dance Pavilion
2704 Avenue O
March 7, 1979, Damaged in a Fire

In 1830, Robert Mills moved from Kentucky to join his brother Andrew in Texas. Here, the brothers engaged in a very successful trading company in Brazoria County. In 1840, Mills moved his base of operations to Galveston Island and purchased out-lot 40, a ten-acre plot of land bounded by Avenues

N and O and Twenty-Seventh and Twenty-Ninth Streets. Mills built a large home on the property and enjoyed his life there. However, due to the Panic of 1873, Mills was forced to declare bankruptcy and relinquish his title to the home and land.

In 1876, a "band of finely nurtured Germans" (according to Julian Ralph in *Harper's Weekly*, 1895) established a social club for the multitude of German immigrants who called Galveston home. That same year, the group purchased Mills's estate and converted his suburban home into its clubhouse. It would also establish a bowling alley and arcade on the property. It would commission August Bader, one of its members, to landscape the property.

Around 1879–80, as noted by the *Galveston Daily News*, the club commissioned a local architect to design a wooden dancing pavilion for the use of its members. The construction of the building began in 1879 and progressed rapidly, as the multitiered, gingerbread-encrusted building took shape, it rose two stories and was eventually topped by a flagpole. This magnificent building was grand in every way. Unfortunately, the architect of the building was never identified. The ornate octagonal dance pavilion is usually credited to the architect Nicholas Clayton, who designed many of the buildings in Galveston at that time. However, it is also possible that the

Garten Verein Dance Pavilion, circa 1897. *Author's collection.*

Galveston Garten Verein, circa 2020. *Author's collection.*

architect was John Moser, a German-born architect who was also practicing in Galveston at that time.

During the 1900 hurricane, the building, as well as many of the park's amenities, were severely damaged. Yet everything was repaired and restored shortly after the storm. The flagpole that originally topped the building was never replaced, and the repairs to the building altered its original roof and the acoustics of the building.

The Garten Verein, a social organization, became a casualty of anti-German sentiment during World War I, and the property and building were sold to Stanley Kempner in 1923. Kempner transferred the property to the City of Galveston to be used as a public park. He asked that it be named for his father, Harris Kempner, and his mother, Eliza Seinsheimer Kempner.

On March 7, 1979, a fire broke out in the northeast corner of the pavilion around 9:20 p.m. The fire department rushed to the scene and worked to put out the flames. In a little over an hour, the fire was extinguished; however, the historic building was severely damaged.

Shortly after the fire, an initial investigation showed signs that someone had been staying beneath the pavilion and may have set the pavilion on fire while trying to stay warm. The investigation uncovered several suspects, including a member of the homeless community and a group of youths who were thrilled by red lights and sirens.

Long after the fire had been put out and the cleanup had started, the true culprit of the fire remained elusive. It wasn't until nearly a year later that a suspect was caught. This suspect was responsible for setting fires at a number of properties near to the pavilion at the time of its fire.

While everyone was sure the pavilion would be restored, the insurance on the building couldn't even touch the true cost of the damage. Eventually, the Moody Foundation stepped in with a grant of $200,000 for the restoration of the building. Early estimates for the restoration and update of the building well exceeded that amount, so multiple bids were solicited and presented ideas on how to repair the building and update it at a lower cost.

By 1981, the building was completely repaired and restored for about $225,000. Today, Kempner Park sits on just a small piece of the original ten acres owned by Mills. Yet it is frequented by locals and visitors alike. Today, the 140-year-old structure serves as an event center for music concerts, weddings, family reunions and other get-togethers.

J. Levy and Brother Funeral Home
2128 Broadway Street
March 30, 1979, Destroyed by Fire, Rebuilt

On Friday, March 30, a fire broke out at the J. Levy and Brother Funeral Home, the oldest funeral home in the state. The funeral home was started in 1868 by Joseph and Benjamin Levy in a small frame building located at the corner of Twenty-First and Church Streets. In 1872, a larger frame structure was located on Church Street, between Twenty-Second and Twenty-Third Streets, and it remained in that location until it moved to its present location in October 1928.

A nearby neighbor stated that, earlier that evening, they smelled smoke; however, they thought it might have been a grass fire that had been burning on Bolivar Peninsula. Later that evening, the smell of smoke was still there but much fainter, so it's thought that the funeral home could have been smoldering for a while before the flames were visible.

The original J. Levy & Bros. Funeral Home on Broadway Street before the fire. *Courtesy of J. Levy & Termini Funeral Home.*

At about 2:08 a.m., the first fire alarm was sounded, and eight pieces of equipment and fifty-six firefighters rushed to the scene. The fire department fought the blaze valiantly until its last vestiges were extinguished. After the fire, inspectors combed the scene, looking for the source of the blaze—which wasn't readily visible.

Eunice Rowe, a longtime resident of the structure who lived on the second floor of the funeral home, was able to escape without injury, but her three dogs died in the fire.

After the fire, the funeral home moved to its temporary headquarters while investigators continued to search for the cause. In April 1979, Fire Chief William Wisko notified reporters that the fire was indeed a case of arson; it had been started in the main parlor, where a can that contained some sort of accelerant was found near the point of origin.

It was estimated that the damages to the home could cost up to $1 million—the only things salvageable being vehicles and records from the business.

On February 16, 1981, J. Levy and Brother moved into its new ten-thousand-square-foot facility, which was built on the site where the previous home had burned.

Washington Hotel
Mechanic Street, at Twenty-Third Street
1983, Destroyed by Fire, Rebuilt

The building that we call the Washington Hotel today started its life as the Cosmopolitan Hotel. The Cosmopolitan Hotel was designed by P.M. Comegy in 1873–74 for John Parker Davie, who was running a successful hardware store at the same location. Along with the hotel, Davie had a structure built next door for his hardware store. After Davie moved the hardware store, the original building was torn down, and construction began on the four-story hotel.

The original building was made of brick covered in stucco to give it the appearance of having white marble stonework. When it was initially constructed, the building, on the first floor, had fanlight transoms over each of its arcade doors and cast-iron lintels and sills on each of its windows. After the June 9, 1877 fire destroyed the original 1839 Washington Hotel, which sat on the corner of Mechanic and Twenty-First Streets, Davie renamed his hotel the Washington Hotel.

Galveston was still cleaning up after Hurricane Alicia when, sadly, on August 26, 1983, at about 12:55 p.m., a fire erupted in the Davie Building, which housed R&B Drugstore. Initially, the flames of the fire were not visible, but the fire, which initially began as a two-alarm fire, quickly gained headway. It quickly gathered strength and soon engulfed the two nearby buildings, one of which was the Washington Hotel. The historic building was vacant at the time, although it was awaiting restoration by George Mitchell. By 3:30 p.m., the flames were erupting from every window of the building.

Within a short time, the ancient brick walls began to crumble and fell to the street below. Black acrid smoke rose high above the structure as the fire continued to surge, destroying more and more of the historic structure. Quickly, the walls began to collapse and sent bricks and other materials crashing to the ground. This caused the firemen and onlookers to scatter. A nearby building, which housed the famed Kon Tiki Club, lost part of its wall to the flames, and power lines in the area were knocked out.

After the fire was finally under control, it was sadly determined that the building was unsafe and would have to be torn down. After several months of investigation, the cause of the blaze was found to have been arson. And estimates of damage ranged from $1.5 million to nearly $2 million.

The Old Washington Hotel, originally the Cosmopolitan Hotel, circa November 1982. *Courtesy of Richard Eisenhour.*

The Washington Hotel ruins after the fire on the corner of Twenty-First and Mechanic Streets. The ruins of the Kon Tiki Club can also be seen. *Courtesy of Richard Eisenhour.*

The burned-out shell of a building that housed the Kon Tiki Club. *Courtesy of Richard Eisenhour.*

Looking down Mechanic Street at the ruins of the Washington Hotel and R.&B. Drugstore. *Courtesy of Richard Eisenhour.*

It seemed that Galveston had lost another piece of its historic fabric. However, George Mitchell, who had originally purchased it with plans of renovating it, decided the building was too vital to the area and said he would indeed rebuild it, preserving as much of the historic structure he could.

Today, anyone who passes by on Mechanic Street once again sees the Washington Hotel and knows nothing of the fire that nearly robbed Galveston of this historic structure.

Moody State School for Cerebral Palsied Children
8900 Teichman Road
Damaged by Fire, Repaired, Relocated 1984

In May 1950, the State of Texas approved a pilot program for a school for children with cerebral palsy. With a gift from William Lewis Moody Jr., the school became a reality and opened in March 1951. It served as a school, rehabilitation center and therapy center in conjunction with the University of Texas Medical Branch.

On June 29, 1956, a faulty air conditioner caused a fire to break out in the occupational therapy room of the building. This prompted forty-five employees and forty-two children to quickly evacuate.

Dorothy Snifflin, who was working with the children in the room at the time, reported the fire and then quickly began to get the children out of the area. They were taken to a garage that was owned by the school and safely away from the flames.

The fire quickly ignited materials beneath a workbench in the room and then moved to a shelf of supplies nearby. Troy Owens, a brace maker for the school, tried to quickly contain the blaze with the fire extinguisher that was in the room. Almost immediately, the flames, heat and smoke became too much, and Owens had to abandon his efforts.

Robertine St. James, the director of the school, stated that all the children were evacuated quickly and without injury. This success was owed to the fact that they had previously practiced a fire drill and Snifflin's quick response in reporting the fire and starting the evacuation proceedings. James stated that considerable damage had been done to the therapy room and adjoining rooms, as well multiple pieces of equipment in the room, but she said she was unsure if the building or equipment was covered by insurance. Thankfully, the damage was contained to a small part of the

Moody State School for Cerebral Palsied Children, circa the 1960s. *Author's collection.*

school, and James said she thought the school would be able to reopen within a week.

Later, James A. Giddings of Austin, the assistant director of the Board of Texas State Hospitals, let James know that men would be sent to evaluate the damage and that there was money to repair and replace the lost equipment.

The only injury reported in the blaze was that of Fire Chief William J. Henderson. He had to get several stitches after breaking through a glass door to escape the smoke in the room where he was trapped. The chief stated that he took his helmet and slammed it against the glass to break it; he apparently nearly fell through, causing him to throw up his arms and receive many lacerations. The smoke in the room, per Chief Henderson, came from burning plastic acetone.

McKinney-McDonald House
926 Winnie Street
1993, Damaged in a Fire

In 1848, Liberty S. McKinney was born in Missouri. In 1874, he married Annie L. Cameron, who was born in Louisiana in 1853. In 1876, Liberty and Annie moved to Galveston, and immediately upon his arrival in Galveston, McKinney became engaged in the wholesale grocery business, which he continued for nearly twenty years. However, in 1898, he began to branch out into the realm of real estate and insurance partnering with J.L. Boeddeker and E.D. Beall.

Around 1889, McKinney built his home in the newly emerging Eastlake style of the period. This home, a raised two-story frame structure with a prominent double gallery, introduced a number of elements that were subtle breaks from the typical style of homes in Galveston at the time. Elements such as the offset gallery, northeast corner wing, front bay and projecting corner pavilions make this home a unique structure on Galveston's historic East End.

Each of the bays display carved friezes and richly modeled details. The house is highly ornamented with three-dimensional details, such as spindles and posts, and the foundation and chimney have elaborate brick molding. The most unique part of the home is its patterned roof, which was once made of slate.

McKinney and Annie moved into the circa 1890 home, though some sources say it could have been built as early as 1888. When all was said and done, the house was finally completed for $3,000. McKinney and Annie had been living in the home about ten years when a devastating hurricane hit the island on September 8, 1900. Liberty and Annie, along with several friends and family, rode out the storm in the home. In 1901, Liberty left Galveston Island and transferred ownership of his home to his business partner, J.L. Boeddeker.

Boeddeker maintained ownership of the home until about 1905, when he sold it to prominent local attorney Dominick McDonald and his wife, Elva. The McDonalds moved into the home in 1905 and did not relinquish ownership of the home until Elva's death on December 7, 1972. After her death, the home was passed from owner to owner until December 1992, when Dr. Bohdan Jarem purchased it and began moving his things in. Shortly after his arrival to the city in October 1992, Dr. Jarem was harassed and had his car vandalized.

On January 8, 1993, the final straw came at noon when smoke was noticed pouring from the attic of the home. For nearly ninety minutes, the fire department bravely fought the fire, finally bringing it under control. Around 9:00 p.m. that evening, the fire department had to return to the home, as embers

A drone photograph of the repaired historic roof design. *Courtesy of Brian M. Davis.*

The restored McKinney-McDonald house, circa 2020. *Author's collection.*

had once again reignited, posing a major threat to the historic structure. After the fire, the home sat vacant, damaged and open to the elements. By 2010, the house was facing demolition if something was not done.

In January 2011, the Galveston Historic Foundation stepped in and purchased the home with its revolving fund. It stabilized the structure and restored the beautiful, patterned roof, saving the home from demolition, weather and vandals. Shortly after, the house was purchased by Angela Mainwaring, who has continued the restoration of this beautiful home. It's hoped that one day soon, the home will be open for tours so that we may all see its grandeur.

Once again, this home stands tall as one of Galveston's rare gems from a nearly forgotten time when the city was one of the most prosperous and wealthiest areas in Texas.

1888 John L. Darragh Home
519 Fifteenth Street
October 1990, Lost Due to Fire

Shortly after Judge John L. Darragh's third marriage to Laura Leonard, the couple bought the property located at 519 Fifteenth Street. The property, at that time, had a few smaller structures, but Darragh and his wife decided to combine these earlier structures to make their new home.

Early records show that Alfred Muller was chosen by the couple to remodel the original buildings on the property and add elements to the home. Slowly, the Darraghs' house began to take shape. The home slowly began to rise to its two-story height; it was crowned by a cupola and framed by two octagonal towers on either side of its double-galleried front porch that faced Fifteenth Street. The home featured a central hall with rooms flanking each side, as well as additional rooms that created an "L" on the rear of the building. The remodel cost $8,000 in 1888.

Mrs. Darragh spared no expense in furnishing her home with luxurious interiors and full carpeting. Muller was even commissioned to create the wrought-iron fence that surrounded the property. Sadly, Judge Darragh, who was suffering from dementia during the construction of the home, enjoyed the home for only a short time. On Wednesday, October 12, 1892, while visiting Massachusetts, Judge Darragh departed this life with his wife by his side.

Mrs. Darragh and her boys remained in the home until 1905, when they leased the property to a number of tenants. It was sold by the Darragh family in 1921, and in 1926, the rear "L" was detached from the home. The rear "L" later became a duplex at 1510 Church Street. The Darragh home took on a new life as an apartment building as well as a fraternity house for the University of Texas Medical Branch.

On December 4, 1985, after the home had sat vacant for nearly ten years, around 6:00 p.m., a twelve-year-old runaway boy set fire to the home while waiting for his friend. Twenty firefighters fought valiantly to save a good portion of the structure; however, the fire and water caused extensive damage to the attic of the home and the octagonal turret.

In March 1986, the Galveston Historical Foundation purchased the home with its revolving fund and planned to stabilize the home for purchase by interested buyers. The home's roof was replaced, and the front porches

The John L. Darragh house, circa 1967. *Courtesy of the Library of Congress.*

The John L. Darragh house after the fire. *Courtesy of Special Collections, Rosenberg Library, Galveston, Texas.*

Darragh Park, the original location of the Darragh home, circa 2018. It was turned into a park after the home burned. The iron fence is original to home. *Author's collection.*

were restored. In 1989, three years after its purchase, the home made its appearance on the 1989 GHF Historic Home Tour.

In September 1990, Bernie and Penny Shaffer purchased the home with plans to restore it to its former glory. Sadly, in October 1990, arsonists once again targeted the home and set fire to the building. The fire was put out, but damage had been done. While the Shaffers were trying to determine the next steps of the home's restoration, arsonists stepped in once again, and this time, they caused so much damage to the home that in April the following year, it was demolished.

Today, the only thing left of the once-grand Darragh house is Darragh Park, which is surrounded by the original wrought-iron fence designed by Muller.

1886 Olympia Freybe/E.S. Levy Building
2227 Postoffice Street
March 13, 1998, Damaged

In 1886, Olympia Freybe commissioned Nicholas Clayton to design a commercial building in Galveston's newly expanded commercial district. On February 26, 1890, Freybe sold her building to Leon Blum for $55,000. In 1917, the clothing firm of E.S. Levy and Company moved from its location on the corner of Market and Twenty-Third Streets to take up residence in the Freybe Building. It was at this time that the building became known as the Levy Building. The original building contained a lot of ornamentation on its exterior; however, over time and after several renovations, much of that ornamentation was lost when the exterior was stuccoed. Also, the canopies that once shaded the sidewalks and patrons of the building were removed.

In 1979, the firm of E.S. Levy closed its doors for the final time, and the building was sold. In 1994, Allen and Carol Naugle purchased the property in the hopes of restoring the building. On the second floor, the Naugles

Looking east down Postoffice Street from Tremont Street, circa 1910. The original Freybe Building can be seen to the right, in the forefront. *Author's collection.*

The Olympia-Freybe Building, located on the corner of Postoffice Street and Twenty-Third Street, circa 2020. *Author's collection.*

had several apartments, and they ran a coffee shop known as Cornerstone Coffees on the first floor.

In March 1998, work began on the building and repairs were made to the elevator shaft to make it usable again. It was determined that the fire began in the elevator shaft. Neither the Naugles nor their tenants realized a fire was raging in the elevator shaft until smoke was noticed by Mrs. Naugle, who was reading at the time. Realizing the severity of the situation, she called the fire department, which responded quickly to the blaze, arriving just moments after she hung up the phone. Immediately, the fire department went about trying to get the blaze under control. The fire destroyed the second-floor apartments of the Freybe Building and burned through the neighboring building's walls and ceiling.

After the fire, the building was restored, returning it to its original appearance. Today, the building looks much like it did before the fire; however, the tenants have changed. Thankfully, though it was threatened, the building was saved and now graces downtown Galveston and provides not only commercial space but also residential space.

Star Drugstore
510 Twenty-Third Street
March 13, 1998, Damaged

In 1886, Kate Scanlon, a member of one of Houston's elite real estate investment families, purchased property in Galveston for the construction of a building in the city's growing commercial district. The original building, designed by Nicholas Clayton, was made entirely of wood and designed to complement its next-door neighbor, the Olympia Freybe Building. Later, in 1906, Charles J. Michaelis purchased the building to be used as a drugstore. He hired J.W. Zempter to change the exterior of the building from wood to brick without destroying Clayton's original design. Three years and $15,000 later, the renovations were complete.

The original Star Drugstore opened in 1890 at the corner of Tremont and Postoffice Streets; however, in 1906, it moved to its current location. Michaelis later added a soda fountain to his pharmacy in 1917. By the 1920s, the building was once again sold to George Clampitt and Grady Dickinson, who operated Star Drugstore until 1982.

Between 1982 and 1998, the building changed hands several times; however, on March 13, 1998, a devastating fire that started in the neighboring Freybe Building nearly destroyed it forever.

Star Drugstore, located on Twenty-Third Street, between Postoffice and Church Streets. *Author's collection.*

The fire moved through the shared wall of the building and burned in the ceiling of the historic building. Reports stated that due to low water pressure and equipment failure, the fire department wasn't able to arrive on the scene in a quick manner. This allowed the fire to burn out of control and gain access to Star Drugstore; however, Fire Chief Danny Webber stated these reports were false, as no bystander could have known what occurred during the blaze.

The building was closed after the fire, and it was not until November 2001 that the Tilts family purchased the damaged building and began a five-year rehabilitation and restoration of it.

The restoration of the building included repairing the façade and building two loft apartments above it. Today, Star Drugstore still prominently faces Market Street with its horseshoe-shaped tile counter and original Coca-Cola sign.

1895 Lloyd S. Downs Home
3202 Avenue N½
July 2, 2016

At 3202 Avenue N½ sits a unique home that was built in 1895 for Lloyd Sanford Downs, MD, and his wife, Mary Alice Johnson. Downs was raised on a farm in Hardin County, Ohio. In about 1880, Lloyd studied medicine in Illinois and Missouri. He married his wife in 1884 and graduated from school in 1885. For a brief time, Downs studied medicine in the Midwest before returning to Texas, settling in the Alta Loma area.

By the 1890s, Lloyd and Mary were in Galveston, where Downs had acquired a teaching position at the University of Texas Medical Branch teaching eclectic medicine. In 1895, he had a home built at 3202 Avenue N½, where he and his family resided. The home is a two-story structure with a partial attic. Inside the home, you will find an entry hall, double parlor, small dining room, kitchen and bathroom on the first floor and three rooms, a bathroom and a small turret-style room on the second floor.

From 1895 to 1914, Dr. Downs and his family enjoyed their home. However, in 1914, they left Galveston to head to Waco, where Dr. Downs continued his practice of eclectic medicine until his death on May 11, 1924.

The house had a number of occupants until it was purchased in 2000 by its current owner and brought back to its former glory. Sadly, in the early

Dr. Lloyd S. Down's home after restoration from the fire, circa 2018. *Author's collection.*

Left: Lloyd S. Downs, MD. *Author's collection.*

Below: View of the Dr. Lloyd S. Downs home after the fire, circa 2016. *Courtesy of Sheri Davis.*

morning hours of July 2, 2016, a fire of unknown origins started on the front porch of the home and quickly swept into the walls and the attic. The fire department responded quickly and extinguished the flames; however, major damage had already been done. The original wavy glass windows had been broken out by the heat; the walls and ceiling were soot-coated; and priceless antiques had been damaged.

For nearly two years, the homeowner and their family and friends worked tirelessly to return this home to its former glory. And due to their diligence and hard work, the home has been repaired and sits shaded among the trees on its historic street within view of the 1838 Menard home.

NOTES

1. In Galveston, "Postoffice" is always written as one word.
2. This description of Campeche is taken from the book *Pirates, Filibusters and Privateers*, by Jean L. Epperson.
3. Harwood, "Colonel Amasa Turner," 37–39.
4. Dr. Greensville S. Dowell was in charge of the Galveston City Hospital and was the founder of the Galveston Medical Society and *Galveston Medical Journal*.
5. Dowell, "Medical Topography," 123–28.
6. Johnston, S. M., *Builders by the Sea: History of the Ursuline Community of Galveston*, pgs. 71–77.
7. The original Washington Hotel was a two-story structure that was located on the corner of Mechanic and Twenty-Second Streets.
8. 1984 Galveston City Directory, xx.
9. 1859 Galveston City Directory, 40.
10. Larry Wygant, "A Sickly City: Health and Disease in Antebellum Galveston, Texas," *Houston Review*, www.houstonhistorymagazine.org.
11. Dowell, "Medical Topography," 127.
12. A rival port city to Galveston that was established on Matagorda Bay was struck by a hurricane on September 15, 1875. It nearly decimated the town, leaving only eight buildings undamaged. A second hurricane, on August 19, 1886, destroyed what remained of the town and filled in its harbor.
13. "Historic House May Unlock Saccarappa Mystery," *Galveston Daily News*, February 26, 1978.

14. Brother of Harbormaster Lent Munson Hitchcock, born in 1817 in Connecticut, died on October 19, 1870, with his wife, Maria, when the steamship *Varuna*, part of the Mallory Lines, sank en route to Galveston. The ship was last seen leaving Florida. When the ship went down, a number of Galvestonians lost their lives, including the Hitchcocks, who left behind a son and daughter. This information was obtained from a newspaper article published in the *New York Times* on November 3, 1870.
15. *History of the Galveston Fire Department*, 59.
16. Ibid., 67.
17. J.S. Brown Hardware Company, originally established by James Moreau Brown. Upon his death, his son John S. Brown took over the management of the store, changing the name. His brother Charles would join the company as vice-president for a brief time.
18. Per the book *Clayton's Galveston*, this building has been known as Weis & Brothers, Block, Oppenheimer and Company and the Galveston Dry Goods Company. This building was designed by Nicholas Clayton in 1881 and was completed in 1882.
19. Miriam and Ira D. Wallach Division of Art, Prints and Photographs Collection, New York Public Library, "Artillery Hall, Galveston, Texas," New York Public Library Digital Collections, www.digitalcollections.nypl.org.
20. Miriam and Ira D. Wallach Division of Art, Prints and Photographs Collection, New York Public Library, "Court House, Galveston, Texas," New York Public Library Digital Collections, www.digitalcollections.nypl.org.
21. The Beach Hotel sat in southeast corner of block number 117, between 23rd and 24th Streets with Avenue Q½ which was not being used at the time passing directly behind it. The back of the hotel would sit directly on the street's edge. A fence circled the entire property with the fence line running down the middle of Twenty-Fourth Street.
22. Port of Galveston appointment calendar for 1978; Robert Nesbitt, "Wilbur Goodman, 90, Takes a Reflective Look at Galveston," 1978, 124.
23. Alazan Heights is in present-day San Antonio.
24. Stewart Mansion is off of Avenue S, Stewart Road, close to 13 Mile Road.

BIBLIOGRAPHY

Archives

Rosenberg Library. Galveston and Texas History Center, 2310 Sealy, Galveston, Texas, 77550.

Websites

Ancestry. www.ancestry.com.
Briscoe Center for American History. www.cah.utexas.edu.
Find a Grave. www.findagrave.com.
Jean Laffite. "Gulf Coast Pirate and Privateer." www.jeanlaffite.net.
Library of Congress. www.memory.loc.gov.
NewspaperARCHIVE. www.newspaperarchive.com.
New York Public Library. www.digitalcollections.nypl.org.
Portal to Texas History. www.texashistory.unt.edu.
Sanborn Fire Maps. www.lib.utexas.edu.
Texas State History Association. "The Handbook of Texas Online." www.tshaonline.org.

Newspapers and Periodicals

Clark, Albert Irving. "The History of Galveston Island 1518–1900." *Bulletin of the University of Texas for Teachers* 14, no. 1 (December 8, 1927): 53–59.

Dowell, Greensville S. "The Medical Topography of Galveston." *Galveston Medical Journal* 1, no. 4 (1866): 123–28.

Fire & Water 19–32 (1896–1902).

Fire & Water Engineering 33–77 (1903–25).

Fireman's Journal 3–18 (1879–86).

Fountain, Kimber. "History of the Galveston Fire Department, Part I: Slate, Shingles and Bucket Brigades, the Early History." *Galveston Monthly* 5, no. 12 (December 2019): 44–46.

———. "History of the Galveston Fire Department, Part II: The Paid Department & Central Station." *Galveston Monthly* 6, no. 1 (January 2020): 34–37.

———. "History of the Galveston Fire Department, Part III: Baptism by Fire—The Great Conflagration of 1885." *Galveston Monthly* 6, no. 2 (February 2020): 32–35.

Galveston Daily News. Various articles. 1841–2012.

Galveston Historic Homes Tour Brochures. Galveston, TX: Galveston Historical Foundation, 1974–2019.

Harwood, Frances. "Colonel Amasa Turners Reminiscences of Galveston." *Quarterly of the Texas State Historical Association* 3, no. 1 (July 1899–April 1900): 44–48.

Morrison, Andrew. *The Port of Galveston and the State of Texas*. St. Louis, MO: G.W. Engelhardt and Company, 1890.

National Fireman's Journal 1–2 (1877–78).

Port of Galveston: America's Port of Quickest Dispatch. Galveston, TX: Chamber of Commerce, 1932.

Port of Galveston, Galveston-Texas. Galveston, TX: Galveston Chamber of Commerce, 1928.

A Riding and Walking Tour of a Residential Community Listed in the National Register of Historic Places. Various revisions and dates of publication. Galveston, TX: East End Historical District Association.

Books and Manuscripts

Alexander, Denise. Images of America: *Galveston's Historic Downtown and Strand District*. Charleston, SC: Arcadia Publishing, 2010.

Barnstone, Howard. *The Galveston That Was*. College Station: Texas A&M University Press, 2008.

Beasley, Ellen, and Stephen Fox. *Galveston Architecture Guidebook*. Houston, TX: Rice University Press, 1996.

Brown, John Henry. *History of Texas*. St. Louis, MO: L.E. Daniell, 1892.

Cartwright, Gary. *Galveston: A History of the Island*. New York: Atheneum, Macmillan Publishing Company, 1991.

Davis, Brian M. Images of America: *Lost Galveston*. Charleston, SC: Arcadia Publishing, 2010.

Dyer, Dr. Joseph O. *The Early History of Galveston*. New York: Springer Publishing, 1916.

———. *The Old Artillery Company of Galve*ston. Galveston, TX: J.O. Dyer, 1917.

Eisenhower, Virginia. *The Strand of Galveston*. Galveston, TX: Privately printed, 1973.

Galveston City Directories. Galveston, TX: various publishers, 1857–1984.

Galveston Fire Department. *History of the Galveston Fire Department: 1843–1906*. Galveston, TX: F.J. Finck Stationary and Print Company, May 1906.

Galveston Historical Foundation's Informational Plaques in the Downtown Historic District.

Gulf Coast Tycoons: The Origin of the Galveston City Company. Galveston, TX: Galveston Historical Foundation, 2016.

Hays, Charles W. *Galveston: History of the Island and the City*. Austin, TX: Jenkins Garrett, 1974.

Johnson, Jan. *Beyond the Beaten Paths: Driving Historic Galveston*. Waco, TX: Eakin Press, 2012.

———. *Walking Historic Galveston: A Guide to Its Neighborhoods*. Waco, TX: Eakin Press, 2009.

Maca, Kathleen. "Remarkable Rescue." *Galveston Monthly* 6, no. 3 (March 2015): 27–30.

McComb, David G. *Galveston: A History*. Austin: University of Texas Press, 1986.

Sardino, Barrie, and Drexel Turner. *Clayton's Galveston: The Architecture of Nicholas J. Clayton and His Contemporaries*. College Station: Texas A&M University Press, 2000.

Turner, Elisabeth Hayes. "Women, Religion and Reform in Galveston, 1880–1920." In *Urban Texas Politics and Development*. Edited by Char Miller and Heywood T. Saunders. College Station: Texas A&M University Press, 1990.

INDEX

A

B

C

D

F

G

H

R

S

T

W

Y

ABOUT THE AUTHOR

Motivated by his own innate curiosity, James F. Anderson has led his life learning through independent studies, research and life experiences. At a young age, he discovered his grandmother's Daughters of the American Revolution application in the family bookcase; it was filled with the names of his ancestors and aroused questions about his lineage. This, along with his love of history and architecture, began his lifelong passion of historical and genealogical research. His interest in research must run in the family, as his grandmother and several ancestors once served as county historians in New York. Throughout his intellectual journeys, his parents have always been his touchstones, encouraging him to seek out hobbies and activities he enjoyed. Based on his faith, James has done just that, leading to a never-ending passion for family, history, architecture and preservation. James was born in the Texas Panhandle and moved extensively before returning to Houston, Texas, in 2004. He became an active volunteer in Houston's Historic Society as a docent during their Christmas Candlelight Tour. In 2007, he discovered Galveston Island, just fifty miles to the south of Houston, and slowly made his transition to the island city. In 2009, he attended a course regarding historic Galveston led by local author Jan Johnson, which firmly established in him a serious case of "Galveston Fever." This caused him to focus his time and research skills on the island city. Since that time, James has honed his speaking skills as a docent at the Bryan Museum and as a tour guide on the Strand and the city cemetery. James joined the Galveston Historical Foundation in 2009, volunteering his time during their annual Historic Homes Tour, of which he became a house chair in 2013. James is currently an active member of the Texas State Historic Association, the Louisiana Trust, the Galveston Railroad Museum and a certified tourism ambassador in Galveston.